Criminal History Record Information Sharing with the Defense Counterintelligence and Security Agency

Education and Training Materials for State, Local, Tribal, and Territorial Partners

DOUGLAS C. LIGOR, SHAWN D. BUSHWAY, MARIA MCCOLLESTER,
RICHARD H. DONOHUE, DEVON HILL, MARYLOU GILBERT,
HEATHER GOMEZ-BENDAÑA, DANIEL KIM, ANNIE BROTHERS,
MELISSA BAUMAN, BARBARA BICKSLER, RICK PENN-KRAUS,
STEPHANIE J. WALSH

Prepared for the Law Enforcement Liaison Office of the Defense Counterintelligence and Security Agency
Approved for public release; distribution unlimited

RAND NATIONAL DEFENSE RESEARCH INSTITUTE

For more information on this publication, visit **www.rand.org/t/RRA846-1**.

About RAND

The RAND Corporation is a research organization that develops solutions to public policy challenges to help make communities throughout the world safer and more secure, healthier and more prosperous. RAND is nonprofit, nonpartisan, and committed to the public interest. To learn more about RAND, visit www.rand.org.

Research Integrity

Our mission to help improve policy and decisionmaking through research and analysis is enabled through our core values of quality and objectivity and our unwavering commitment to the highest level of integrity and ethical behavior. To help ensure our research and analysis are rigorous, objective, and nonpartisan, we subject our research publications to a robust and exacting quality-assurance process; avoid both the appearance and reality of financial and other conflicts of interest through staff training, project screening, and a policy of mandatory disclosure; and pursue transparency in our research engagements through our commitment to the open publication of our research findings and recommendations, disclosure of the source of funding of published research, and policies to ensure intellectual independence. For more information, visit www.rand.org/about/principles.

RAND's publications do not necessarily reflect the opinions of its research clients and sponsors.

Published by the RAND Corporation, Santa Monica, Calif.
© 2022 RAND Corporation
RAND® is a registered trademark.

Library of Congress Cataloging-in-Publication Data is available for this publication.

ISBN: 978-1-9774-0973-7

Cover: kali9/Getty Images/iStockphoto.

Limited Print and Electronic Distribution Rights

This document and trademark(s) contained herein are protected by law. This representation of RAND intellectual property is provided for noncommercial use only. Unauthorized posting of this publication online is prohibited. Permission is given to duplicate this document for personal use only, as long as it is unaltered and complete. Permission is required from RAND to reproduce, or reuse in another form, any of its research documents for commercial use. For information on reprint and linking permissions, please visit www.rand.org/pubs/permissions.

About This Report

The U.S. Department of Defense (DoD) Defense Counterintelligence and Security Agency (DCSA) is the federal agency responsible for conducting the background investigations and personnel vetting for 95 percent of the federal workforce, including current and prospective federal government employees and contractors. DCSA collects relevant criminal history record information (CHRI) as part of these investigations from federal and state, local, tribal, and territorial (SLTT) law enforcement and criminal justice agencies. SLTT organizations, however, are often unaware of DCSA's role and responsibilities and unaccustomed to CHRI collection and federal background investigations generally. This lack of awareness can impede or delay DCSA's collection of CHRI. In turn, it can slow the investigation and vetting process for federal employees and contractors.

To help address this challenge, Congress authorized DCSA to provide training and education assistance to SLTT communities in 2020 to streamline and improve access to historical criminal record data. DCSA then requested assistance from the RAND Corporation's National Defense Research Institute (NDRI) with developing educational and training materials to use in support of these activities. The objective of these materials is to develop and deepen SLTT agencies' knowledge and understanding of their federal statutory obligations to share CHRI with DCSA and to facilitate more effective and efficient CHRI sharing. The materials are also intended to help create a more robust partnership between DCSA and the more than 18,000 law enforcement and criminal justice agencies nationwide. The materials contained in this report and the underlying research conducted to build the materials are the fulfillment of this request.

The research reported here was completed in April 2022 and underwent security review with the sponsor and the Defense Office of Prepublication and Security Review before public release.

RAND National Security Research Division

This research was sponsored by DCSA's Law Enforcement Liaison Office (LELO) and conducted within the Forces and Resources Policy Center of the RAND National Security Research Division (NSRD), which operates the National Defense Research Institute (NDRI), a federally funded research and development center sponsored by the Office of the Secretary of Defense, the Joint Staff, the Unified Combatant Commands, the Navy, the Marine Corps, the defense agencies, and the defense intelligence enterprise.

For more information on the RAND Forces and Resources Policy Center, see www.rand.org/nsrd/frp or contact the director (contact information is provided on the webpage).

Acknowledgments

We thank the leadership of DCSA's LELO—in particular, Dan Leary, Mark Pekrul, and David Hicks—for their assistance at all phases of this project and for sharing their expertise, experience, and insights. We also thank DCSA's Special Agents-in-Charge, investigators, and headquarters and field staff who shared their expertise and facilitated our connection to key SLTT and other law enforcement personnel.

We also wish to thank Sina Beaghley for her contributions to the project and review of the training materials, Craig Bond for his review, and John Bordeaux and Bob Harrison for their careful peer review of the report. Additionally, we would also like to thank Stephanie Holliday for providing us with a review of sources to support the development of our learning theory analysis. Finally, we would like to thank Kayla Howard for coordinating and tracking federal and SLTT interactions and all her administrative support throughout this project.

Summary

Issue

As part of the conduct of background investigations, the U.S. Department of Defense's Defense Counterintelligence and Security Agency (DCSA) collects criminal history record information (CHRI) from federal and state, local, tribal, and territorial (SLTT) law enforcement and criminal justice agencies. SLTT organizations, however, are often unaware of DCSA's role and responsibilities, CHRI collection, and federal background investigations generally, which can impede or delay the investigation and vetting process.

To help address this challenge, Congress passed legislation in 2020 authorizing DCSA to provide training and education assistance to SLTT communities for the purpose of streamlining and improving access to historical criminal record data. To assist DCSA in responding to this congressional requirement, the project team conducted research to meet two overarching objectives: (1) assess the current educational and training needs of SLTT law enforcement agencies (LEAs), and (2) develop education and training materials to address current gaps related to CHRI reporting compliance by SLTTs.

Approach

To develop and design the training materials, the research team took a multistep approach that included a review of DCSA resources related to mission, objectives, programs, policies, and procedures; a review of open-source literature on law enforcement training; interviews with DCSA managers and staff and SLTT LEA personnel; and a review of broader adult training and education literature, from which we applied the prevailing learning theories (i.e., self-directed learning, experiential learning, and andragogy). We then developed training materials using appropriate design and branding before sending them to both DCSA and SLTT personnel for review. Feedback from the reviews was used to make improvements in the education and training materials as they were finalized.

Key Findings

From our research, and particularly from interviews with DCSA and SLTT staff, we identified processes and procedures for, and impediments to, CHRI sharing; informational gaps; and problems with current DCSA materials that informed our development of the education and training materials. Key insights include the following:

- Current and past materials have inconsistent branding—often using branding of the prior organizations that carried out the background investigative mission before DCSA (i.e., Office of Personnel Management and National Background Investigations Bureau)—which creates confusion for SLTT LEA personnel.
- Current and past materials contain information gaps that result in confusion or lack of understanding by SLTT LEAs regarding DCSA's mission, responsibilities, authorities, procedures and processes, and CHRI needs.
- CHRI is not defined consistently by federal and SLTT LEA personnel, which results in different interpretations of what information is covered and, in turn, what information SLTTs are willing to share.

- Interpersonal skills matter. Forming and maintaining relationships with SLTT LEA personnel (leaders, managers, and staff) is an important aspect of CHRI sharing.
- A diverse set of training materials that can be used in different circumstances (such as a presentation for a training seminar or conference, compared with a one-pager for a short interaction with an SLTT LEA desk sergeant) would best meet DCSA's needs.
- DCSA and SLTT LEA personnel are trained on CHRI information sharing via different venues; education and training materials need to be useful for a variety of circumstances (such as face-to-face meetings, email, and remote online interactions).
- DCSA staff could use materials to educate SLTT LEA personnel about their legal obligation to provide CHRI to DCSA.

Recommended Education and Training Materials

The RAND team used the above insights in addition to concepts of adult learning theory to develop a new suite of education and training materials for DCSA. The suite contains the following eight components:

1. *CHRI Sharing Guidebook*: A comprehensive baseline document that addresses all facets of CHRI sharing for SLTT LEAs, including how to effectively and efficiently partner with DCSA.
2. *Frequently asked questions*: Information in a question-and-answer format drawn from the most frequently reported issues and questions raised by SLTT LEA personnel.
3. *Fact sheet*: A concise summary of critical DCSA and CHRI sharing points designed for meetings and conversations that DCSA personnel have with SLTT LEA personnel in various circumstances.
4. *One-pagers* (three versions): Very brief distillations of DCSA, its authorities, and CHRI sharing procedures designed for circumstances where time is very limited.
5. *Brochures* (two types): Short informational documents designed to cover all major points from the CHRI Sharing Guidebook.
6. *Email*: Introduction of DCSA to SLTT LEAs.
7. *Training presentation*: Revised version of DCSA's current training presentations designed to accommodate various SLTT audiences and be delivered in a variety of settings.
8. *Posters* (five versions): Various distillations of DCSA, its authorities, its inquiry forms, and CHRI sharing procedures designed for distribution and public display at SLTT LEAs and large-scale gatherings, such as conferences, seminars, and education and training events.

Contents

About This Report iii
Summary v

CHAPTER ONE
Introduction 1
    Approach 3
    Methodology Framework 3
    Organization of This Report 4

CHAPTER TWO
Review of DCSA Materials 5
    Document Review Process 5
    Key Elements and Considerations 6

CHAPTER THREE
Learning Styles for Law Enforcement Audiences 11
    Foundational Learning Theories 11
    Law Enforcement Learning Environments 16

CHAPTER FOUR
Insights from the Stakeholder Community 19
    Branding 19
    CHRI Definition 19
    Interpersonal Skills 20
    Modality 22
    Strategy for Uncooperative Locations 23
    Trainings 23
    Other Suggestions 24
    Conclusion 24

CHAPTER FIVE
Development of the Education and Training Materials 25
    Drafting and Revision of the Final Education and Training Materials: Pilot Field Testing 26
    Conclusion 30

APPENDIX
A. Methodology Framework 31
B. CHRI Sharing Guidebook 37
C. Frequently Asked Questions 79
D. Fact Sheet 85
E. One-Pagers 89
F. Brochures 95
G. Email 103
H. Training Presentation 105
I. Posters 117

Abbreviations 123
Bibliography 125

Figures and Tables

Figures

2.1.	Non-DCSA Branding Example	8
2.2.	Law Check Template Examples	9
3.1.	Police Foundation Survey on Officer Safety Training	17
5.1.	Field Testing Feedback Collection Form	27

Tables

3.1.	Materials to Learning Theory Mapping Matrix	12
3.2.	Andragogy Versus Pedagogy	15
4.1.	Exemplar Quotations on Branding	20
4.2.	Exemplar Quotations on CHRI Definition	20
4.3.	Exemplar Quotations on Interpersonal Skills	21
4.4.	Exemplar Quotations on Modality	22
4.5.	Exemplar Quotations on Strategy for Uncooperative Locations	23
4.6.	Exemplar Quotations on Trainings	24
4.7.	Exemplar Quotations on Other Suggestions	24
5.1.	Exemplar Quotations from Pilot Field Testing	28
A.1.	Framework Elements for the Fact Sheet	31
A.2.	Framework Elements for Frequently Asked Questions	32
A.3.	Framework Elements for the Training Briefing	32
A.4.	Framework Elements for Posters	33
A.5.	Framework Elements for Brochures	33
A.6.	Framework Elements for Email	34
A.7.	Framework Elements for One-Pagers	34
A.8.	Framework Elements for Guidebook	35
A.9.	Mapping Learning Objectives to DCSA Training Materials	36

CHAPTER ONE

Introduction

The Defense Counterintelligence and Security Agency (DCSA) is the federal agency responsible for conducting the background investigations and personnel vetting for 95 percent of the federal workforce, including current and prospective federal government employees, the U.S. military, and government contractors. As part of this mission, DCSA is required to collect all relevant criminal history record information (CHRI) on individuals for whom it is conducting background investigations. This information is critical for DCSA to assess and adjudicate issues involving suitability, fitness, and the eligibility of individuals to access sensitive and/or classified information and hold positions of trust and sensitivity within the U.S. government.[1]

Access to, and the collection of, CHRI is substantially dependent on the capability and willingness of state, local, tribal, and territorial (SLTT) law enforcement and criminal justice agencies to respond to DCSA requests for CHRI in accordance with their federal statutory obligations.[2] Many SLTT agencies, however, are not aware of DCSA, its mission and authorities, or the processes and procedures associated with sharing CHRI with DCSA. This knowledge gap can impede or delay the ability of SLTT agencies to comply with CHRI requirements.[3] To mitigate this challenge, Congress enacted Section 1625(b) of the National Defense Authorization Act for Fiscal Year 2020, which authorizes the Director of DCSA to "carry out a set of activities to reduce the time and cost of accessing State, local, and tribal law enforcement records for background investigations required for . . . Federal Government employees and contractors."[4] The set of activities "shall include only that *training, education*, and direct assistance to State, local, and tribal communities needed for the purposes of streamlining access to historical criminal record data" (emphasis added).[5]

To assist DCSA in carrying out its responsibilities with respect to the education and training of SLTT law enforcement and criminal justice agencies, we conducted research to meet two overarching objectives:

1. Assess the current education and training needs of SLTT law enforcement agencies.

---

[1] DCSA defines *suitability* as a person's character or conduct that may have an impact on the integrity or efficiency of the individual's government service; *fitness* as the adjudicative decision made on excepted service, contractor, and other federal personnel working for or on behalf of the federal government; and *security clearance eligibility* as a determination that a person is able and willing to safeguard classified national security information and/or occupy a national security–sensitive position. Suitability, fitness, and national security adjudications have unique principles and guidelines under which their respective adjudicative decisions are made. See DCSA, "Adjudication," webpage, undated.

[2] See U.S. Code, Title 5, Section 9101, Access to criminal history records for national security and other purposes ("Upon request by a covered agency [such as DCSA], criminal justice agencies [i.e., Federal, State, or local court or agency, or any subunit thereof] shall make available all criminal history record information regarding individuals under investigation. . . ").

[3] B. Goggins and D. DeBacco, *Challenges and Promising Practices for Disposition Reporting*, report from the 2017 SEARCH Winter Membership Group Meeting, Phoenix, Ariz., January 24–26, 2017, pp. 2–3.

[4] Section 1625, Defense Counterintelligence and Security Agency activities on facilitating access to local criminal records historical data, of Public Law 116-92, National Defense Authorization Act for Fiscal Year 2020, December 20, 2019.

[5] Pub. L. 116-92, 2019, Section 1625(b).

2. Develop education and training materials to address current gaps related to CHRI reporting compliance by SLTTs and design the materials to enable the effective distribution and communication of these materials from DCSA personnel to the appropriate SLTT law enforcement and criminal justice agency personnel.

This report addresses objective one by describing and detailing our assessment of the current education and training environment for SLTT agencies. The report also addresses the first part of objective two by providing drafts of the developed education and training materials. We addressed the second part of objective two by designing the materials to enable effective deployment to SLTT LEAs.

To meet the two objectives, the RAND Corporation team executed three tasks:

Task 1: Understand and analyze the "as-is" education and training environment as it applies to compliant and noncompliant SLTT law enforcement agencies (LEAs). We conducted a review and analysis of DCSA documentation, data, and other information related to the rates of compliance of SLTT LEAs in response to requests for CHRI. We also conducted more than 50 interviews with DCSA and SLTT leaders, managers, and personnel to further inform this analysis. In doing so, we ascertained the characteristics (or causes, if determinable) for both SLTT LEA failures and successes in complying with CHRI requests that related to issues of education and training.

Task 2: Analyze and determine education and training needs. We analyzed the results of Task 1 and determined both the current best practices and the current gaps related to SLTT LEA education and training for the purposes of CHRI response. As part of this analysis, the team identified best practices, factors, techniques, tools, and other mechanisms that facilitate both CHRI access and sharing.

Task 3: Develop education and training materials for SLTT LEAs to facilitate DCSA's access and collection of CHRI. Based on the analysis performed in Task 2, and the prevailing literature on adult learning and effective training approaches and techniques for law enforcement personnel, we developed a suite of eight education and training materials:

- *CHRI Sharing Guidebook*
- frequently asked questions (FAQ)
- fact sheet
- one-pagers (three versions)
- brochures (two styles)
- email introduction of DCSA to SLTT LEAs
- training presentation
- posters (five versions).

To the extent practicable, these materials are in a format that allows for remote access and/or remote presentation and instruction. It is anticipated that DCSA would likely send these materials electronically and make them available in hard copy through all its field offices.

Task 4: Pilot test and revise materials. During the final phase of the project, we piloted the materials with select DCSA field offices and SLTT LEA jurisdictions, soliciting feedback through structured written forms. We incorporated the feedback from this effort into the final materials presented in Appendixes B through I. In support of the second part of objective two, we designed the materials to enable effective deployment, application, and use for the purpose of educating and training SLTT LEAs.

Approach

To support the development and design of our training materials, we took a multistep approach that included the following:

- a review of materials provided by DCSA that included internal and external documents related to the agency; its mission and objectives; and its programs, policies, and procedures. We supplemented this extensive background information with information available on DCSA's public website, including such agency publications as *DCSA Gatekeeper* and *DCSA ACCESS*.[6]
- a review of open-source material on law enforcement education and training (from various jurisdictions), including that which is specific to training officers and other law enforcement personnel regarding background investigations and vetting.
- 50 interviews with DCSA managers and staff (including field Special Agents, Special Agents-in-Charge, investigative assistants, and other field office and regional office personnel) and SLTT LEA personnel to understand their experiences related to CHRI collection and sharing.
- a review of the education and training literature, including standard methods and manners of delivering law enforcement education and training. For this report, we address our selected literature review as it applies to the development of our methodology framework described in the following section.

Methodology Framework

To integrate the information collected from the various sources described in the previous section, we developed a methodological framework that would assist us in (1) using the information from DCSA source materials and interviews efficiently and effectively, and (2) applying the most-applicable learning theories to the development of the education and training materials. Essentially, the framework serves as a checklist for the components that should be included throughout the education and training material curriculum. For instance, each education and training material should address and/or incorporate the following:

- a learning objective (i.e., Who is DCSA? How is DCSA organized? What authorities does DCSA have?)
- a learning theory (i.e., self-directed, experiential learning; andragogy)
- a particular audience (i.e., patrol officers, records staff, court clerks)
- the type of material (i.e., one-pager, briefing, FAQ)
- designated topics covered (i.e., DCSA history, CHRI requests and definitions, investigator procedures)
- recommended messaging (i.e., national and public security, state laws superseded by federal laws, increased understanding of the waiver process)
- excerpts from the DCSA source material and/or interviews conducted.

The framework elements for each education and training material are detailed in Chapters Three through Five and in Appendix A. Generally, we determined that a broad approach was required when applying applicable learning theories to the development of the education and training materials. The objective of the project—to develop materials to improve CHRI sharing between DCSA and SLTT LEAs—is unique. Both the subject matter (federal-SLTT CHRI sharing) and DCSA's relationship to the audience (as a requester of

---

[6] See, generally, *DCSA Gatekeeper* issues at U.S. Department of Defense, Defense Visual Information Distribution Service, "Defense Counterintelligence and Security Agency," webpage, undated-b; and *DCSA ACCESS* issues at U.S. Department of Defense, Defense Visual Information Distribution Service, *DCSA ACCESS Magazine*, online portal, undated-a.

information from the various levels of SLTT leaders, managers, and staff across approximately 18,000 SLTT law enforcement jurisdictions) do not lend themselves to standard types of education or training environments, e.g., classrooms, academies, and similar institutional environments where education and training would occur in a structured manner over a designated period.

In the literature reviewed, no analogues to the training dynamic applicable here are examined or discussed. Most law enforcement education and training are classroom-based, which is not a practical option for DCSA to employ. As a result, we adapted existing learning activities to best fit the unique circumstances presented by the relationship between DCSA and its mission and the SLTT LEA community's role in sharing CHRI requested by DCSA. For example, we developed materials that facilitate quick, self-directed learning, self-paced online learning, or short face-to-face briefings or instruction. Some of the materials, such as the training briefing, could be used by DCSA or SLTT agencies in an adult-learning-based setting with opportunities to engage the audience when appropriate.

Organization of This Report

This report provides a brief overview of how our data collection and analysis supported the creation of new education and training materials for DCSA. The following chapters describe the results of our document review and analysis and our collection and analysis of interview data. Both sources of data and evidence informed the topics, subject matters, items for inclusion, and formats selected for the suite of education and training materials.[7]

We begin in Chapter Two with a discussion of our review of DCSA's current organizational and training materials, followed in Chapter Three by an overview of law enforcement learning styles. In Chapter Four, we report the findings from our interviews and how these findings informed the development of the education and training materials. In the final chapter, we describe the eight types of training materials developed. These materials are then presented in Appendixes B though I.

---

[7] To produce the deliverables, we were also provided with current marketing schemas and branding requirements from DCSA.

CHAPTER TWO

Review of DCSA Materials

As the first step in our research, we conducted a review and analysis of training, organizational, and informational materials from DCSA related to CHRI and personnel vetting. We conducted the review to better understand the processes and procedures employed by DCSA to train investigators and to assess the materials used in their training. The following describes our process and highlights key considerations that informed the development of the new training materials.

Document Review Process

Overall, DCSA provided 85 documents for our review. These included the following:

- current education and training materials used for DCSA field staff and SLTT audiences (briefings, brochures, one-pagers, and other similar training aids) related to personnel vetting
- DCSA internal education and training materials from the DCSA National Training Center (e.g., Background Investigator Skills Standards and Core Competencies)
- the *Federal Investigative Standards*,[1] the *Investigator's Handbook*,[2] and the Federal Background Investigator Training Program materials
- data collection form (INV Form 44) sample
- DCSA organizational materials (e.g., internal command presentations and briefings, organizational charts, and others)
- DCSA CHRI collection and sharing policy memoranda, standard operating procedures, and guidance documents
- DCSA/SLTT formal and informal correspondence regarding CHRI collection and sharing
- criminal justice and CHRI collection and sharing reports from various federal and state entities, as well as private law enforcement associations and research organizations
- congressional and U.S. Government Accountability Office (GAO) materials
- court documents and other criminal justice agency materials (e.g., training, operating procedures, and vetting processes and procedures).

We conducted a review and analysis of these documents to determine what existing information could be included in the new education and training materials. Our goal was to distill and select the information, facts, modalities, and other relevant data that, when incorporated into the new materials, would provide

---

[1] U.S. Office of Personnel Management, *Federal Investigative Standards*, v.5, September 14, 2020, Not available to the general public.

[2] U.S. Office of Personnel Management, *Investigator's Handbook*, Federal Investigative Services Division, July 2007, Not available to the general public.

DCSA with an effective mechanism to improve CHRI collection and sharing with SLTT LEAs. These documents contained information about DCSA, its organization, its mission, background investigations, CHRI, processes and procedures for collecting CHRI, and the SLTT LEA jurisdictions with which DCSA engages. Therefore, it was necessary to carefully review the documents to isolate information, facts, modalities, and other data applicable to educating and training SLTT personnel to improve CHRI sharing.

To accomplish this, we examined and analyzed these documents to answer the following key questions:

- How could this information be used to inform the training that we develop for state and local law enforcement and court agencies?
- Should this information be included in the training? Could it help inform the types or formats of training that we develop?

Next, the team examined and performed a qualitative analysis of each document to understand how it might support and inform new education and training materials. This step included identifying the following fields and then distilling and selecting any examples or references from the documents related to these fields:

- general descriptions or summaries of what a DCSA investigator does and its relation to national security
- types of CHRI that DCSA requires for federal background investigations
- types of training materials that are or have been used by DCSA
- types of training modes (i.e., in-person classes, webinars, self-guided instruction, and others) used by DCSA
- information that other DCSA offices, divisions, and centers (i.e., the National Training Center) share about CHRI and interacting with state and local agencies
- challenges that SLTT agencies face in providing CHRI to DCSA that we should include and/or should try to address in our training materials
- relevant cases or examples of incidents that could have been prevented with better CHRI sharing between SLTT agencies and the federal government.

Key Elements and Considerations

This broad review and analysis revealed several key elements related to topics, substantive material, specific items and factual points, formatting, branding, and consistency that were critical for framing new education and training materials. First, the review highlighted multiple types of potential formats for our training materials. For example, the documents included the following formats specific to training or education materials: briefings, training scripts, Word/PDF documents, sample LEA or court records, sample email queries to SLTT LEAs, step-by-step guidebooks, brochures, and one-page information sheets. Additionally, we were provided with a DCSA training presentation and script for investigators that are not available to the general public. While this presentation was not directly pertinent to the substantive content included in the materials for SLTT LEA personnel, it contributed to the creation of companion notes for use with the SLTT LEA training presentation.[3]

---

[3] We did not incorporate any publicly unavailable materials in the creation of the SLTT LEA training presentation or in any of the developed training materials because one of the goals of the project was to create materials that could be disseminated as widely as possible.

Second, some materials provided a wealth of relevant information related to CHRI sharing. Two presentations from DCSA's Law Enforcement Liaison Office (LELO) created for LEAs and DCSA field staff were especially important to the development of our materials. Interview data indicated that the topics and substantive information included in these presentations were effective. Thus, information from these current tools helped frame the set of topics, factual elements, and CHRI sharing impediments we included in the new materials.

Third, repeated information within the DCSA documentation informed our selection of covered topics. Regarding specific topics and substantive material, information extracted consistently focused on CHRI—its definition, the various types of CHRI produced by criminal justice agencies, and the processes and procedures employed by DCSA for its collection and use. As a result of the emergence of these key elements, we designed specific types of materials (e.g., a briefing, a fact sheet, a revised brochure, an email message blast, and posters) that addressed specific substantive material and factual points of order (e.g., how CHRI is defined, specific examples of CHRI, DCSA investigator procedures, DCSA statutory authorities).

Finally, we identified inconsistencies in how DCSA materials were branded and presented within different levels and offices. In terms of branding the materials, we observed discrepancies between the agency's current name (DCSA) and what was printed on agency documentation, materials, and forms, which often still include references to the legacy Office of Personnel Management (OPM) or the National Background Investigations Bureau (NBIB). Figure 2.1 contains an example.

We also found that individual investigators developed their own templates and materials, which varied across DCSA Field Offices and Regional Office jurisdictions. For example, in outreach to SLTT LEAs, the letterheads and approaches to introduce the agency (e.g., as an agency of the U.S. Department of Defense [DoD]) differed. These materials led to confusion among SLTT LEA personnel regarding DCSA—even in cases in which tools were reported as effective by DCSA staff. Such inconsistencies are demonstrated in Figure 2.2. As a result of this finding, we ensured that the entire suite of new education and training materials would have common branding that SLTT LEAs would recognize.

FIGURE 2.1
Non-DCSA Branding Example

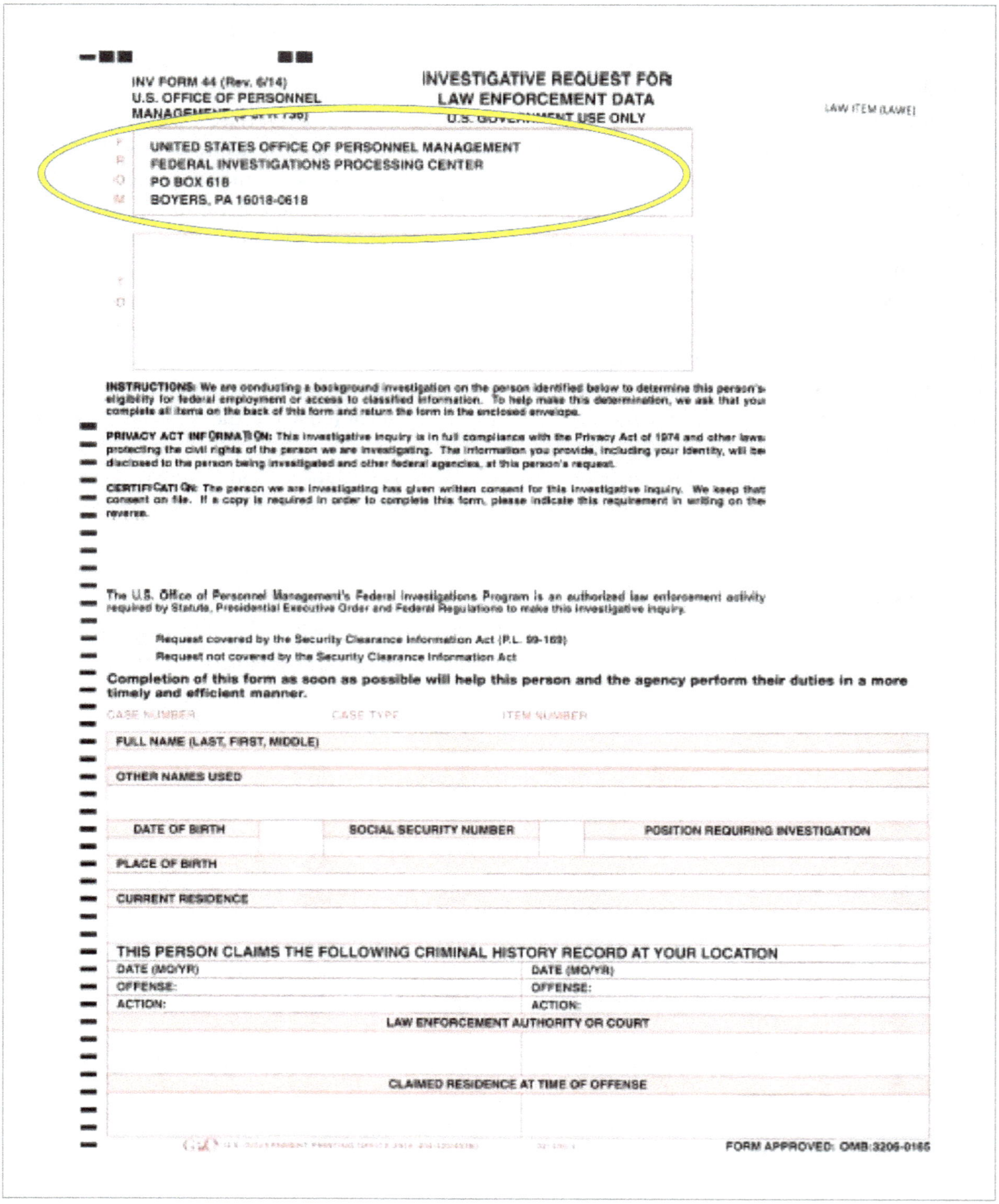
INV FORM 44 (Rev. 6/14)
U.S. OFFICE OF PERSONNEL MANAGEMENT

INVESTIGATIVE REQUEST FOR LAW ENFORCEMENT DATA
U.S. GOVERNMENT USE ONLY

LAW ITEM (LAWE)

UNITED STATES OFFICE OF PERSONNEL MANAGEMENT
FEDERAL INVESTIGATIONS PROCESSING CENTER
PO BOX 618
BOYERS, PA 16018-0618

INSTRUCTIONS: We are conducting a background investigation on the person identified below to determine this person's eligibility for federal employment or access to classified information. To help make this determination, we ask that you complete all items on the back of this form and return the form in the enclosed envelope.

PRIVACY ACT INFORMATION: This investigative inquiry is in full compliance with the Privacy Act of 1974 and other laws protecting the civil rights of the person we are investigating. The information you provide, including your identity, will be disclosed to the person being investigated and other federal agencies, at this person's request.

CERTIFICATION: The person we are investigating has given written consent for this investigative inquiry. We keep that consent on file. If a copy is required in order to complete this form, please indicate this requirement in writing on the reverse.

The U.S. Office of Personnel Management's Federal Investigations Program is an authorized law enforcement activity required by Statute, Presidential Executive Order and Federal Regulations to make this investigative inquiry.

Request covered by the Security Clearance Information Act (P.L. 99-169)
Request not covered by the Security Clearance Information Act

Completion of this form as soon as possible will help this person and the agency perform their duties in a more timely and efficient manner.

CASE NUMBER CASE TYPE ITEM NUMBER

FULL NAME (LAST, FIRST, MIDDLE)
OTHER NAMES USED
DATE OF BIRTH | SOCIAL SECURITY NUMBER | POSITION REQUIRING INVESTIGATION
PLACE OF BIRTH
CURRENT RESIDENCE

THIS PERSON CLAIMS THE FOLLOWING CRIMINAL HISTORY RECORD AT YOUR LOCATION
DATE (MO/YR) DATE (MO/YR)
OFFENSE: OFFENSE:
ACTION: ACTION:
LAW ENFORCEMENT AUTHORITY OR COURT
CLAIMED RESIDENCE AT TIME OF OFFENSE

FORM APPROVED: OMB:3206-0165

SOURCE: DCSA.
NOTE: Non-DCSA name (OPM) is highlighted in yellow.

FIGURE 2.2
Law Check Template Examples

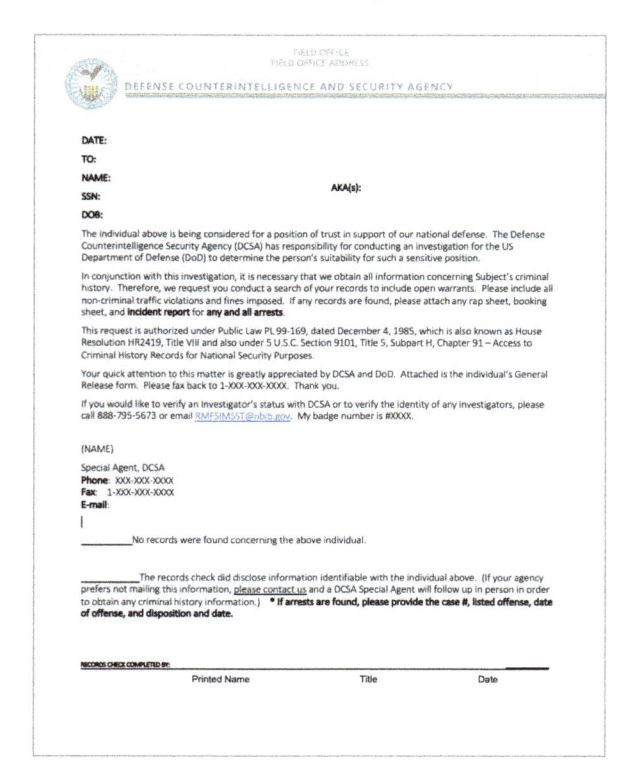

SOURCE: DCSA.
NOTE: Any investigator or field office identifying information has been anonymized from these examples.

CHAPTER THREE

Learning Styles for Law Enforcement Audiences

The underlying goal is for SLTT LEAs to work effectively with DCSA investigators—recognizing that, in practice, there will be a number of nuances and questions that will arise within each agency. Due to time, resource, effectiveness, and other jurisdictional and authority constraints,[1] DCSA cannot mandate its trainings across LEAs. In place of a nationwide mandated DCSA training session, we focused on equipping DCSA personnel with materials to educate and train LEA staff in a manner consistent with the conditions of their interactions and the nature of their relationships. We also focused on providing LEA staff with the information that they need to share CHRI with DCSA effectively and efficiently. The materials—in the form of brochures, posters, and other media—are designed both to improve the level of partnership between DCSA and SLTT LEA personnel and to increase the awareness and understanding of CHRI sharing obligations among LEA staff. The development of these materials is based on learning theories and environments successful in law enforcement communities.

Foundational Learning Theories

As a starting point to achieve the project's goals, we conducted a search of the most effective and engaging learning theories that have been successfully used among law enforcement officers and concepts that may be adapted to the particular LEA environment in which DCSA operates. We selected the following learning approaches to serve as the foundation of the learning strategies embedded throughout our training materials: self-directed learning, experiential learning, and andragogy. These are seminal adult learning theories that, although distinct, share several overlapping principles that serve to strengthen the learning process: *self-directed learning* allows individuals to choose a particular task they would like to learn, as well as the methods by which to learn it; *experiential learning* applies real-life experiences to training and development; and *andragogy* acknowledges and respects the unique experiences (and stressors) within an adult work environment. Table 3.1 contains a mapping of the learning theories as they apply to the individual training materials that we developed. It is important to note that, although each material is mapped to an individual learning theory, many of the tailored materials may also overlap with other learning theories. For instance, although a material may be identified as a self-directed material, it may also include some element of andragogy. Table 3.1 is a summary of the principal learning theory that applies to a specific training material.

The development of specific training materials, guided by the needs of DCSA and SLTTs, provide only a limited opportunity for the full use of learning styles described below. For example, there is no need for in-person, scenario-based training for SLTTs to understand how to interact with DCSA investigators. Rather, this can be accomplished through simpler means of outreach using many of the training materials. We also

---

[1] 5 U.S.C. 9101 does not provide DCSA with the authority to mandate or compel SLTT LEAs to undergo or participate in DoD/DCSA-directed CHRI sharing training. Thus, all the training materials were developed to facilitate voluntary participation by SLTT LEAs.

TABLE 3.1
Materials to Learning Theory Mapping Matrix

Materials	Learning Theories		
	Self-Directed Learning	Experiential Learning	Andragogy
One-pager 1	X		
One-pager 2	X		
One-pager 3	X		
Fact sheet		X	
FAQ			X
Poster 1	X		
Poster 2	X		
Poster 3	X		
Poster 4	X		
Poster 5	X		
Guidebook	X		
Brochure 7 x 9	X		
Brochure trifold	X		
Email			
Training briefing		X	

leave space for interaction in the training presentation for discussion and "what-if" scenarios that accommodate different learning styles. Similarly, because of the often-busy operational tempo at SLTTs, we developed concise materials that can be quickly referenced and that the end-user can absorb on their own time, allowing for some *self-direction*.

Self-Directed Learning

Self-directed learning posits that adults need to be actively involved in their learning process by providing a flexible structure, collaboration opportunities, and choice and control over learning and their specific learning objectives. It is also particularly suited to adult professionals who can set their own learning goals, locating appropriate resources, deciding how to learn with or without the support of others, and evaluating their progress. "The characteristics of self-directed learners include independence, willingness to take initiative, persistence in learning, self-discipline, self-confidence, and the desire to learn more."[2]

---

[2] K. Cercone, "Characteristics of Adult Learners with Implications for Online Learning Design," *AACE Journal*, Vol. 16, No. 2, 2008, p. 148.

An important facet of self-directed learning is that the locus of control lies within the adult learner—that they are choosing their learning objectives and have agency over their learning experience.[3] Students have more agency over what, how, where, and when they learn—and there is an element of flexibility that allows accommodation for the lives of students. An example would be online programs that allow students to choose course loads that work with their schedules.[4]

The value of self-directed learning is demonstrated when students successfully achieve objectives by following their own directives to problem solve and learn. Students use their own troubleshooting skills to meet an immediate need and answer their questions. Officers would identify their own knowledge gaps around a certain topic—such as "Does DCSA need parking violation information?" or "What level of detail in CHRI does DCSA need from our department exactly?"—and be able to identify appropriate resources to answer this question. Self-directed learning is embedded in the way officers navigate the DCSA materials. To encourage this type of decisionmaking, departments could also foster practice opportunities that present complicated real-life DCSA scenarios, reinforcing intuition and self-evaluation processes.[5]

Self-directed learning is the principal learning theory in the majority of the training materials: "Sharing CHRI with DCSA" (one-pager 1); "Collaborating with DCSA to Ensure Public Safety and National Security" (one-pager 2); "DCSA CHRI Sharing 101" (one-pager 3); "Sharing CHRI with DCSA" (brochure 7 x 9); "Criminal Justice and the U.S. Department of Defense" (brochure trifold); "Filling out INV Form 44 for Federal Employee Background Check" (poster 1); "Background Investigations" (poster 2); "How to Help with Background Investigations Conducted by the DCSA" (poster 3); "Responding to DCSA Requests" (poster 4); and "Federal Background Checks" (poster 5).

These materials highlight the following core learning objectives:

- Who is DCSA?
- What does DCSA do, and how does its duties relate to national security?
- What is DCSA interested in?
- What authorities does DCSA have?
- What does the law require?
- What should you do if DCSA contacts you?
- What forms and methods are used by DCSA?

Table A.9 in Appendix A elaborates on the objectives covered by each type of training material.

Experiential Learning

Adult learners have a variety of lived experiences, and experiential learning leverages these experiences as a learning mechanism. "In simplest form, experiential learning means learning from experience or it's learning by doing."[6] The main components of experiential learning comprise (1) knowledge of experiences and facts, (2) prior knowledge of events, and (3) reflection and assessment and its potential contribution to indi-

---

[3] C. M. Lowry, "Supporting and Facilitating Self-Directed Learning," *ERIC Digest*, No. 93, 1989.

[4] P. Beach, "Self-Directed Online Learning: A Theoretical Model for Understanding Elementary Teachers' Online Learning Experiences," *Teaching and Teacher Education*, Vol. 61, 2017; S. Vonderwell and S. Turner, "Active Learning and Preservice Teachers' Experiences in an Online Course: A Case Study," *Journal of Technology and Teacher Education*, Vol. 13, No. 1, 2005; S. B. Merriam and L. L. Bierema, *Adult Learning: Linking Theory and Practice*, San Francisco: Jossey-Bass, 2014.

[5] Cercone, 2008, note 9.

[6] L. H. Lewis and C. J. Williams, "Experiential Learning: Past and Present," *New Directions for Adult and Continuing Education, 1994*, Vol. 62, 1994, p. 5.

vidual development.[7] Experiential learning enables linkages between personal development, work, and education.[8] This approach aims to use students' learned experiences from the past, connect them to their present experiences, and reflect on future implications.[9]

Experiential learning was selected because it is participative, interactive, and applied. Further, experiential learning values a learning environment focused on the practical issues of a profession where instruction can be applied directly to the students' daily duties and responsibilities. Students often learn through "hands-on" instruction; they learn by performing specific skills. Such learning allows contact with the environment in which the adult professional learner is located and exposure to highly variable and uncertain processes. This learning theory values the years individuals spend in various LEA positions and numerous trainings. It also values any professional certifications that they have earned and uses the added skill sets gained through each professional position they have held.

Ultimately, these prior experiences are leveraged to assist professional and personal development through experiential learning. For example, by following instructions on how to verify DCSA federal and contractor credentials, as described in the training materials, LEA personnel will become adept at these procedures, allowing for more efficient sharing when DCSA or contractor personnel change. Experiential learning is the principal learning theory in two of the training materials—"Sharing CHRI with DCSA" (fact sheet) and "DCSA Information Sharing for National Security" (training briefing)—because these materials provided a more in-depth look at the relevant processes in comparison with the self-directed materials, which examine specific topics only "at-a-glance." For instance, with experiential learning, agents can review the specifics of CHRI, what it encompasses, background, and potential contacts. In doing so, agents may use their past interactions with sharing CHRI with DCSA or other entities, check their knowledge of the different procedures, and learn where their gaps of understanding may lie. These materials also highlight all the core learning objectives. Table A.9 in Appendix A contains a detailed mapping of the objectives covered throughout each education and training tool.

Andragogy

A key principle of andragogy is that adult learners need to know why they need to learn something. "Explaining the purpose of the assignment and the learning outcome of the assignment prior to assigning a task can increase the chance that the adult learner will be motivated to attempt the task."[10] Andragogy is rooted in the belief that adult students are more inclined to be motivated when they understand what they are expected to learn.[11]

The fundamental tenet of andragogy is that adults and children have different learning traits and characteristics, as shown in Table 3.2.[12] It is important to note that although *pedagogy* is mainly associated with

---

[7] Cercone, 2008, note 10.

[8] D. A. Kolb and L. H. Lewis, "Facilitating Experiential Learning: Observations and Reflections," *New Directions for Continuing Education*, Vol. 30, 1986.

[9] S. B. Merriam and R. S. Caffarella, *Learning in Adulthood*, 2nd ed., San Francisco: Jossey-Bass, 1999.

[10] C. Cochran and S. Brown, "Andragogy and the Adult Learner," in K. Flores, K. D. Kirstein, C. E. Schieber, and S. G. Olswang, *Supporting the Success of Adult and Online Students*, Scotts Valley, Calif.: CreateSpace, 2016.

[11] Cochran and Brown, 2016.

[12] M. S. Knowles, *Self-Directed Learning: A Guide for Learners and Teachers*, New York: Association Press, 1975.

TABLE 3.2
Andragogy Versus Pedagogy

Andragogy	Pedagogy
Self-directed learner	Learner dependent on decision of teacher
Larger amount of life experiences	Few life experiences
Learning needs closely related to social roles	Learning needs dictated by the teacher
Problem-centered	Subject- and content-centered
Intrinsically motivated	Extrinsically motivated

SOURCE: B. W. Wambeke, B. E. Barry, and J. C. Bruhl, *Teaching Model as a Living Document*, 2017 ASEE Annual Conference and Exposition, Columbus, Ohio, June 24–28, 2017.
NOTE: This table, from research conducted at the U.S. Military Academy, West Point, outlines key distinctions between teaching adults (*andragogy*) and teaching children (*pedagogy*).

teaching children, given certain circumstances, it may also apply to teaching adults. For instance, a pedagogical approach would apply to an adult learner with no background in a particular topic.[13]

The theory of andragogy acknowledges that as a person grows and matures, their self-concept "changes from that of a dependent personality toward that of a self-directed individual."[14] Adults tend to come into adult education activities with a greater volume and higher quality of experience than younger children. Adult learners, particularly adult professionals who are required to learn new information or new ways of approaching a problem, tend to be ready to learn things that they believe they need to know or do to cope effectively with real-life situations and problems. Knowles' theory of andragogy has also received some criticism over the past few decades. Some claimed ideas presented in andragogy are merely good practices for learning and lack an empirical basis.[15] Others believe that andragogy inaccurately assumes that all adult learners have a similar background and learning preferences (i.e., self-directed learners).[16]

An example of andragogy in practice is when an adult learner tries to become better at their job: They realize that by applying this new skill set, they will do their job more effectively. They have determined that there is a problem in how things are being done, and they are able to take a step back and be motivated to learn something new because it will make their job easier.

Andragogy is a useful principle in this instance because we were tasked with designing materials for adults in various law enforcement and related records capacities and at different levels of experience (e.g., supervisor, new employee). So, for example, in the case of learning about DCSA's authorities, the materials allow LEA personnel to learn the basics, such as only the list of records that constitute CHRI under the statute, or they can dig deeper into the statute (5 U.S.C. 9101), Executive Orders, or regulations to develop a more fulsome understanding of DCSA's vetting functions. Andragogy is the principal learning theory driving the FAQ because that tool was created to assist an SLTT user who is motivated to solve a problem in the workplace. See Table A.9 in Appendix A for a detailed mapping of the objectives covered throughout each tool created.

---

[13] V. McGrath, "Reviewing the Evidence on How Adult Students Learn: An Examination of Knowles' Model of Andragogy," *Adult Learner: The Irish Journal of Adult and Community Education*, Vol. 99, 2009, p. 110.

[14] Cercone, 2008, note 10.

[15] S. B. Merriam, "Andragogy and Self-Directed Learning: Pillars of Adult Learning Theory," *New Directions for Adult and Continuing Education*, Vol. 89, 2001, p. 3.

[16] Merriam, 2001, p. 3.

Law Enforcement Learning Environments

Typical police or law enforcement training (or educational) settings involve significant classroom time, anchored in a traditional pedagogy.[17] The most significant portion of training occurs when recruits are in the various academies, although there are recurring trainings that are mandated by agencies, state oversight commissions, and legislation. In addition, LEA personnel may attend outside training opportunities, whether to fulfill the hours necessitated by their state's Peace Officer Standards and Training (or equivalent), to become a member of a particular unit (e.g., SWAT, Explosive Ordnance Disposal), or for general professional development.

There have been recent pushes to incorporate more adult learning concepts in the classroom in comparison with previous training models, often focusing on the academy level.[18] In context, these recent efforts echo many past studies and recommendations on police training and the need for contemporary and relevant adult training methods.[19] These recommendations spring not only from adult learning and education theory, but from ideas on what might provide officers tools for policing in a 21st-century democracy.[20]

A survey conducted in 2020 by the National Police Foundation found that classroom lecture and online training were the two *least preferred* methods of instruction for police officer safety training (Figure 3.1).[21] Higher scores, such as those for scenario-based, virtual reality, and interactive classroom training, represent higher levels of preference for these training techniques. While these approaches may not apply to all types

---

[17] See, e.g., D. Bradford and J. E. Pynes, "Police Academy Training: Why Hasn't It Kept up with Practice?" *Police Quarterly*, Vol. 2, No. 3, 1999; M. R. McCoy, "Teaching Style and the Application of Adult Learning Principles by Police Instructors," *Policing: An International Journal of Police Strategies & Management*, 2006; J. Connolly, "Rethinking Police Training," *Police Chief*, Vol. 75, No. 11, 2008; J. R. Oliva and M. T. Compton, "What Do Police Officers Value in the Classroom? A Qualitative Study of the Classroom Social Environment in Law Enforcement Education," *Policing: An International Journal of Police Strategies & Management*, 2010; and R. H. Donohue and N. E. Kruis, "Comparing the Effects of Academy Training Models on Recruit Competence: Does Curriculum Instruction Type Matter?" *Policing: An International Journal*, 2020. Drawing on this literature, we also note that, for new hires—such as a new records clerk—pedagogy is appropriate, since it is well suited to adults approaching new material for the first time. See, also, the testimony of Erik Bourgerie, Director, Colorado Peace Officers Standards and Training (POST): "More important than the number of training hours required is the quality of training offered. Unfortunately, many academy and in-service training programs rely on lecture-based learning. We know that this teaching method is not as effective in teaching adult learners, but it is less expensive than the better alternatives. Improving the quality of this fundamental training will increase overall performance by peace officers. While lecture-based training may be appropriate for certain, limited topic areas, it's vital for the law enforcement profession that we move away from this teaching methodology to embrace modern, evidence based adult learning concepts" (Erik J. Bourgerie, written testimony for the President's Commission on Law Enforcement and the Administration of Justice, U.S. Department of Justice, May 13, 2020).

[18] D. Stoika, moderator, "President's Commission on Law Enforcement and the Administration of Justice," conference call transcript, U.S. Department of Justice, May 13, 2020; D. M. Blumberg, M. D. Schlosser, K. Papazoglou, S. Creighton, and C. C. Kaye, "New Directions in Police Academy Training: A Call to Action," *International Journal of Environmental Research and Public Health*, Vol. 16, No. 24, 2019, p. 4941.

[19] M. L. Birzer and R. Tannehill, "A More Effective Training Approach for Contemporary Policing," *Police Quarterly*, Vol. 4, No. 2, 2001; M. L. Birzer, "The Theory of Andragogy Applied to Police Training," *Policing: An International Journal of Police Strategies & Management*, 2003; McCoy, 2006, note 28; G. Cleveland and G. Saville, *Police PBL: Blueprint for the 21st Century*, U.S. Department of Justice, Office of Community Oriented Policing Services and Regional Community Policing Training Institute at Wichita State University, 2007.

[20] For example, officers need to practice such concepts as strong communications skills, critical thinking, and problem-solving. See O. Marenin, "Police Training for Democracy," *Police Practice and Research*, Vol. 5, No. 2, 2004; and E. P. Werth, "Scenario Training in Police Academies: Developing Students' Higher-Level Thinking Skills," *Police Practice and Research*, Vol. 12, No. 4, 2011.

[21] J. Rojek, J. Grieco, B. Meade, and D. Parsons, *National Survey on Officer Safety Training: Findings and Implications*, Washington, D.C.: National Police Foundation, 2020.

FIGURE 3.1
Police Foundation Survey on Officer Safety Training

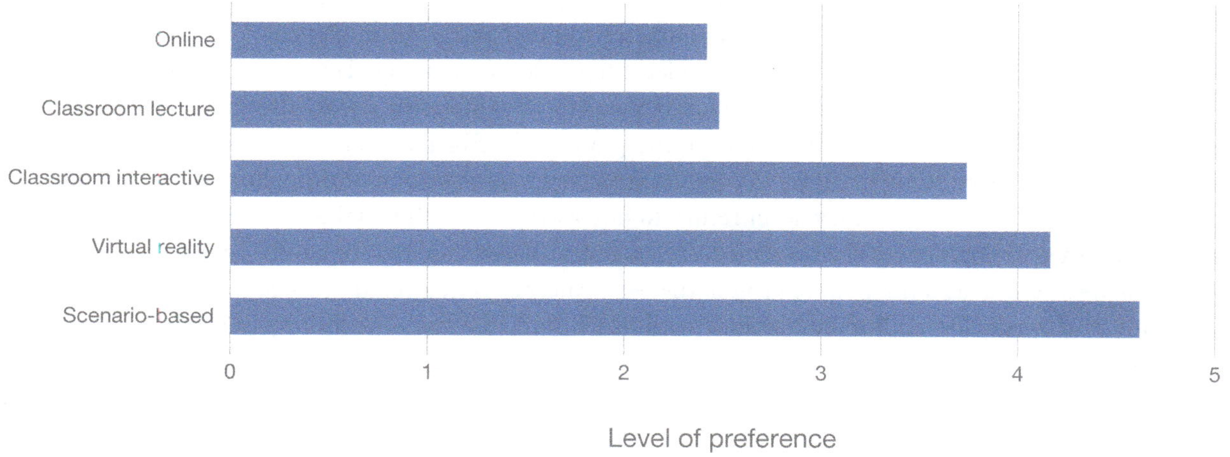

Training Type	Level of preference
Online	~2.4
Classroom lecture	~2.5
Classroom interactive	~3.7
Virtual reality	~4.2
Scenario-based	~4.6

SOURCE: Rojek et al., 2020.
NOTE: Survey scores range from 1 (low preference) to 5 (high preference).

of training, the survey results further strengthen the idea that LEA personnel prefer hands-on or interactive training.

The coronavirus disease 2019 (COVID-19) pandemic altered law enforcement training beginning in the spring of 2020, whether it be by the temporary closures of police academies, limiting training, shifting courses online, or a combination of approaches. Some of these alterations and changes remain in effect in some jurisdictions as of the writing of this report. INTERPOL shifted to a virtual setting to provide training modules in over 100 self-paced courses.[22] State Peace Officers Standards and Training (POST) organizations suspended or canceled classroom instruction or moved classes online.[23] Although it is unclear how long online training will remain a fixture across the spectrum of training topics, it should be a familiar concept across law enforcement.

Even prior to the increase in the application of online delivery methods resulting from the COVID-19 pandemic, the move to online learning and training for LEA personnel, as in other sectors, had been growing. The federal government, through direct support from the Community Oriented Policing Services (COPS) office and other sources, offers a variety of training modules for federal and SLTT personnel. COPS E-Learning stresses that it is a time- and cost-efficient resource.[24] Federal resources are also supplemented by other public and private offerings, including those at the state level[25] and vendors such as PoliceOne Acad-

---

[22] INTERPOL, "INTERPOL Launches Virtual Academy to Support Police Learning During COVID 19," press release, April 29, 2020.

[23] These have been tracked at International Association of Directors of Law Enforcement Standards and Training, "Academy Policies and Procedures in Time of Pandemic," webpage, undated.

[24] For COPS e-learning course offerings, see Community Oriented Policing Services Training, "E-Learning," webpage, undated.

[25] State POSTs or others may integrate training into online offerings for initial or in-service training. For example, Connecticut offers in-person and virtual offerings. See Connecticut State Police Officer Standards and Training Council, "In-Service Training Courses," webpage, 2021.

emy.[26] In another example, Federal Law Enforcement Training Centers' (FLETC) *Strategic Plan 2018–2022* stated that one of their objectives is to "expand and strategically employ e-FLETC, FLETC Talks, and other distributed learning capabilities to achieve maximum impact within the law enforcement community."[27] This use of online materials allows for broader outreach to more and larger audiences.

Considering these aspects of law enforcement learning styles, we developed education and training materials that, while attempting to be as consistent as possible with effective styles, also factor in the unique environment in which DCSA's education and training outreach efforts will take place. For example, DCSA personnel will not have the opportunity to conduct structured, in-classroom training for set lengths of time. In fact, most SLTT jurisdictions may never return to in-classroom training as the primary learning environment. Thus, the development of classroom lectures, scenario-based modules, or hands-on practical exercises would not be as useful as it might have been in the past. Alternatively, given that DCSA personnel will likely have limited time during ad hoc interactions with SLTT staff, the use of summary and other short-form materials (such as one-pagers, FAQs, fact sheets, and short presentations) is the most effective method for knowledge development in various SLTT jurisdictions.

---

[26] For PoliceOne Academy courses, see PoliceOne Academy, homepage, undated.

[27] Federal Law Enforcement Training Centers, *Strategic Plan, 2018–2022*, Glynco, Ga., undated, pp. 21 and 42.

CHAPTER FOUR

Insights from the Stakeholder Community

To further inform the creation of our materials, we conducted semistructured interviews with subject-matter experts at DCSA and the SLTT LEAs. The interviews yielded important information on processes and procedures for CHRI sharing, relationship building, current impediments to information sharing, and how to best inform, educate, and train SLTT LEA personnel to share CHRI with DCSA. From our interviews, we identified seven high-level themes—branding, CHRI definition, interpersonal skills, modality, strategy for uncooperative locations, trainings, and other suggestions—and compiled quotations to illustrate the sentiments expressed during these discussions. This chapter contains details for each of the identified themes.[1]

Branding

We define *branding* as clear, consistent material pertinent to DCSA as the federal agency lead for federal workforce background investigations. Through our interviews and document review, we discovered material, emails, and logos that used OPM or NBIB branding rather than DCSA. Interviewees reported that this issue causes confusion among SLTT LEA personnel. Consequently, our materials address this concern and explain DCSA's history and name changes to convey the legacy relationship between OPM, NBIB, and DCSA. Table 4.1 includes exemplar interviewee quotes on branding differences.

CHRI Definition

Our interviews also revealed some confusion, concern, and even pushback on what was defined as CHRI generally, and what that definition meant practically (Table 4.2). For example, the federal definition of CHRI refers to "identifiable descriptions and notations of arrests, indictments, informations, or other formal criminal charges, and any disposition arising therfrom, sentencing, correction supervision, and release."[2] DCSA personnel interpret this clause to include items such as police reports, logs, and other documented interactions with subjects, whether or not the interaction has led to a formal arrest and booking and/or criminal disposition before a court of law.

Many SLTT LEA personnel, however, do not consider CHRI to include interactions with subjects that, while documented in some manner, do not result in an actual arrest or booking. DCSA and SLTT LEA interviews expressed that many states and localities have their own definition of CHRI, and these definitions do not always align with the federal definition or the interpretation of the federal definition applied by DCSA

---

[1] Among these themes, we do not address exogenous factors, such as lack of SLTT LEA funding or resourcing (staff and equipment). Although these themes came up in many of the interviews, we did not include them as a point of analysis because they focus on SLTT LEA concerns that are unlikely to be affected by DCSA outreach education and training materials.

[2] 5 U.S.C. 9101(a)(2).

TABLE 4.1
Exemplar Quotations on Branding

Interview Number	Quotation
7	"It was two years since we became DCSA from NBIB. In my email, I would put in 'formerly NBIB.' I went to [Masked Name Police Department] with [Masked Name] to meet with them when we changed our name to DCSA to give them a heads up. With [Masked Name record system], some of the PDs required IR numbers for OPM, and they were asking for the number on faxes. Do you know our IR number is still OPM?"
9	"When I was newer, I definitely looked at and read one-pagers. It's not great when you introduce yourself as DCSA and your email says NBIB."
10	"We don't have a standardized letter across the agency, so every agent creates his own."
	"They don't understand why they get five different agents faxing them five different requests with five different letterheads."
22	"Nothing comes to mind for me [for introducing DCSA and CHRI sharing], and I haven't heard of an agent asking for more. Brochures are professionally made, informative, and [have] contact information on there. We have electronic versions, which I think is great."

SOURCE: RAND interviews.
NOTE: IR = individual reference; PD = police department.

TABLE 4.2
Exemplar Quotations on CHRI Definition

Interview Number	Quotation
3	"When they title it as CHRI, everyone has a different definition of that. I am working with a PD right now and he said do not put CHRI. That means something completely different and means public access. That is not giving you the incident report and the full case narrative. It is communicating with the PD and obtaining from them how they need us to request it."
	"The only bad thing about Title 5 is that it refers to CHRI which feds define differently than how locals might define."

SOURCE: RAND interview.
NOTE: PD = police department.

staff. Given these definitional anomalies, our education and training materials include the full federal definition of CHRI and DCSA's interpretation of this definition (in the form of specific types and categories of CHRI). We emphasize these distinctions throughout all our materials.

Interpersonal Skills

During our interviews, the importance of forming and maintaining relationships with SLTT LEA personnel (leaders, managers, and staff) was stressed as an important facet of CHRI sharing. Table 4.3 contains examples of what we heard from interviewees. While the new education and training materials are not intended to teach interpersonal skills to DCSA or LEAs, they are designed in a manner to facilitate understanding and connection between DCSA and SLTT LEAs, both institutionally and personally (between investigators

TABLE 4.3
Exemplar Quotations on Interpersonal Skills

Interview Number	Quotation
7	"You can go meet and greet also and establish rapport with the police departments. If I am going to a particular place, I had an address book. If I walk into a place, I already knew who the person at the front desk was. Once they know who you are, you can walk right in. Follow-up is excellent."
	"During that time, the agents were faxing it in. You can imagine we do a lot of background investigations here in [Masked Name city]. I wanted to come up with a simpler way in order to get those law checks done as soon as possible. I spoke to my area chief about talking to [Masked Name Police Department]. I took over some donuts and coffee to thank them for quickly responding to our faxes. When I went over, I asked to meet with their record supervisors so we can make it a lot simpler to gather and obtain information from them. We spoke with them and took [Masked Name] with us and they gave us access to their system. Not only does [the Masked Name record] system cover [Masked Name City], but they also cover other areas."
20	"There are brochures but have only provided [them] when there have been issues. COVID threw a wrench in what we were providing. It's rare in [our area] that the person we're contacting doesn't know us, unless they have a new hire. [Our area] is less formal and thrives on relationships."
23	"Also timing matters [on delivering outreach training to SLTTs]. If you're there getting records, it's a bad time to do that because they are trying to serve lots of people. If there was someone who was dedicated to training, that would be better. We used to have LELO positions that did outreach, which was good, but it's also good to have a local POC [point of contact]. In law enforcement, people follow chain of command. It would be good for a supervisor to establish a relationship, although it is not necessarily up to them to maintain it."
25	"Taking the brochure, leaving the business card, trying to keep friendly, open communication with them has been helpful."
32	"Most of them go on trying to get rapport with the people. Once you have a friendship, you go forward, explaining why we need what we need. Once you get someone on your side, we share that [the brochure]."

SOURCE: RAND interviews.

and SLTT personnel).[3] For example, we designed the one-pagers to help a DCSA investigator quickly communicate key informational elements about DCSA and CHRI to SLTT LEA personnel in instances in which they may only have a few minutes to interact, such as when the SLTT official is on duty at a records reception window. The one-pagers take these circumstances into account and are designed to support the initial formation of a CHRI sharing partnership between DCSA and the SLTT LEA. In this respect, the training materials should serve as important mechanisms for outreach, discussion, and rapport building, which are all essential elements for CHRI collaboration and sharing.

---

[3] DCSA could consider adding training and education to its National Training Center program related to outreach, professional relationship building, and trust building to enhance interactions between frontline DCSA personnel and SLTT personnel. This may also be an area for further research. Additionally, we note that changes in behavior within organizations also invite the opportunity for change management, which is designed to address barriers to relationship building, biases, or other impediments to cooperation. See, generally, C. Bellavita, ed., *How Public Organizations Work: Learning from Experience*, New York: Praeger, 1990; and C. Heckscher, *The Collaborative Enterprise: Managing Speed and Complexity in Knowledge-Based Businesses*, New Haven, Conn.: Yale University Press, 2007. DCSA may also consider further research in this area to address the CHRI sharing enterprise more generally.

Modality

We asked our interview participants what kind of training materials they believed would be best suited for the broad set of SLTT LEA audiences. The ideas and feedback provided in response (see Table 4.4) were the main driver for the types of materials that we created for DCSA (e.g., a presentation that could also be used for an online webinar or at a conference, and a fact sheet that could be used to describe DCSA and the need for CHRI sharing to an SLTT LEA desk sergeant or other records supervisor with limited available interaction time).

TABLE 4.4
Exemplar Quotations on Modality

Interview Number	Quotation
3	"We do have one pamphlet we received this week. We can potentially send it out electronically; it wasn't formatted right to do that. That does explain everything and has a lot of great information."
5	"The less you give them, the shorter the ask, the more direct, the better."
9	"Standardization among materials, particularly letterheads and standard letter and shorter materials that provide [information] at a glance regarding DCSA."
10	"We used to have fairly decent pamphlets; not a fan of the current one, which is not a trifold. Some of our guidance is out of date."
	"Maybe just a quick info sheet that doesn't cite too much or [is] too informative like a piece of paper with bunch of letters on it. Short and sweet information on who we are and a footer or something that says you should be providing this info."
11	"I don't think it is necessarily bad. But a lot of times, I may be going to a place where it's the first time they've dealt with us. The current one [brochure] is way too long. I want something that I can pull out while I am there that explains who I am and what I am doing. Maybe provide some numbers if they want some more information. Right now, it's a two-page pdf document. I just want the bottom line. They are not going to read that while I am in line to get the record."
13	"One-pager I like. Separate from PowerPoint of course. Short direct to point. Good enough. Don't overwhelm. Not too much info. Enough to explain. (Presentation better for a crowd.)"
15	"Prior to changing to NBIB, we had pamphlets; just got new ones. They're laughable—no one's going to read it. Now they're not even printed. We present credentials (required), state our purpose, sometimes people nod (they know the routine). Just showing the badge, introducing themselves."
17	"I wish I had materials that go with the booth, training material/pamphlet. They should be generic so it works for the next person in line from me. CD would be the easiest way to distribute material."
22	"I don't think the FAQ or a fact sheet would hurt. I think we got a great brochure. Depending on what you are trying to communicate, it might be buried in there. In the electronic version of the brochure, I often highlight one or two sentences in there to help them pinpoint what we are talking about. If there is something that might supplement those brochures, it would be great, especially if it is accessible to everybody on the DCSA website. I don't know if the brochures are linked and available to the public. If an agent could refer a department to this website that looks pretty official and has information specific to LEAs, I could see that being a benefit."
35	"I think it would be very beneficial if there was a webinar or a PowerPoint we can share with any new and current employees. I think just providing information on what it is and how it came about and who is authorized with all the background information should be very helpful."
37	[In response to whether leave-behinds would be effective.] "Yes, something simple that lines out what we should expect to see and get back."

SOURCE: RAND interviews.

Strategy for Uncooperative Locations

Interview highlights for this theme focus on how investigators or other DCSA staff can use education and training materials to overcome obstacles or further inform SLTT LEA personnel as to their legal obligation to provide CHRI to DCSA. Table 4.5 includes exemplar quotations on the use of training materials to address challenges with uncooperative locations. Each of our recommended training materials incorporates several focus points to address these obstacles and issues, e.g., Title 5 of the U.S. Code, Section 9101 explanations (of DCSA's jurisdiction, authorities, and the federal statutory definition of CHRI), streamlined emphasis on public safety and national security linkages, opportunities to obtain legal opinions from state and local authorities, and providing access to local records management systems and databases.

TABLE 4.5
Exemplar Quotations on Strategy for Uncooperative Locations

Interview Number	Quotation
2	"If a place they go to isn't cooperative, we used to give them the law enforcement brochure—have been told they're being worked on and are awaiting legal review. Most recent version is 2017, [we] were NBIB at the time. Also have a compliance letter we make sure all the new agents receive to try and help elicit cooperation."
11	"What do you do whenever you aren't hearing from people, and they aren't following up? Sometimes we will call our SAC [Special Agent-in-Charge] and our SAC will call them up. If it is in person, I will hand out the brochure."
20	"Making it easier on them. We are not the only person asking them for stuff. Alleviating their workload is a message I think would resonate. When they gave [DCSA staff member] access to their system . . . she could say 'if you give me access to your system, you don't have to do it.' Beyond that, there's an element of national security, but I don't know how much weight that would give. These are small towns where folks have worked 25 years . . . I don't know how motivated they are based on the legal obligation to comply."
23	"I haven't seen one [uncooperative SLTT jurisdiction] where the pamphlet changed someone's mind."
24	"All they care about is if you have a release. I'm sure they're already trained that way. If you have a release and a badge, there are no problems. I never had a problem in all my years in the field."
31	"In those cases, the onus is on the agent to respectfully inform them why they are required to provide the information. We make sure our agents inform them about Title 5. The Feds were supposed to let LEAs know about it, including contract side of the house. I don't think that message got to all LEAs. If an investigator is told no and just walks away, we've lost the opportunity to educate the LEA about Title 5. It may take time. They may want to talk to their attorneys, etc. That's fine. Investigators need to be willing to do that and be patient: 99.9 percent of the time if you do that, you get what you need."

SOURCE: RAND interviews.

Trainings

The training theme underscores how DCSA and SLTT LEA personnel are trained on CHRI sharing, and when and how the education and training materials should be distributed, applied, and used by DCSA. We focused on this theme to determine the level of familiarity with potential education and training materials for SLTT LEA personnel. Table 4.6 includes exemplar interview statements related to this concern. Since the SLTT LEAs that we examined had never developed education and training materials to specifically address the sharing of CHRI between the two types of entities, we developed materials that could be used to educate and train both DCSA personnel and SLTT LEA personnel. For example, the materials could be used by DCSA supervisors in the field to help educate and train new DCSA investigators who are recent FLETC graduates assigned to their offices.

TABLE 4.6
Exemplar Quotations on Trainings

Interview Number	Quotation
2	"Have thousands of documents for curriculum. It would be helpful for us to see snippets of how we feature people who collect law enforcement records. Can also look at national training standards."
11	"Now when you are hired, you go directly to the academy. Before, you were with a trainer for 30 days and shadowed him."
	"You went to training and you felt like you actually practiced the introduction. You went to the academy and when you came back, you were put with your mentor for two weeks and they would follow you out and just let you do the interviews and make recommendations."

SOURCE: RAND interviews.

Other Suggestions

Lastly, we included and analyzed a number of general or unique comments that did not neatly fit into any of the other themes, but that we believed to be both informative and helpful in the development of our materials and that are responsive to DCSA and SLTT LEA personnel needs, expectations, and capabilities (Table 4.7). For example, several interviewees indicated how important it is that DCSA investigators properly and consistently identify themselves when initiating first contact with new SLTT LEAs. Thus, we ensured that the training materials aligned with the appropriate and approved techniques for DCSA investigator interactions with outside entities.

TABLE 4.7
Exemplar Quotations on Other Suggestions

Interview Number	Quotation
3	"One of the major points was that the records we receive should not just be what they provide with public access. We are considered an agency that should be receiving the information. If they could explain to their staff, which doesn't always happen where the chief talks to their record division and claim to them that DCSA is not a public record check and are looking for any information on the subject we can get. Giving us a narrative of the incident is a must."
9	"I start with 'I am [name], Special Agent with the Defense Counterintelligence and Security Agency. It is a federal agency under DoD that does national security and trust investigations.'"
10	"Most agents refrain from identifying themselves as DoD [in] some way. The automatic assumption is you are a recruiter of some type."
15	"Agent that maintains a database of all employers in [Masked Name city]. Any time we get a new POC, he updates the database."

SOURCE: RAND interviews.

Conclusion

The information gleaned from key stakeholder interviews was an essential part of the process of identifying gaps in education and training, including related materials, that we could address in developing the new set of education and training materials. We did so by consistently incorporating the identified themes throughout the suite of materials.

CHAPTER FIVE

Development of the Education and Training Materials

As stated in the previous chapters, we used the insights gleaned from our review of DCSA and related documents, interviews with stakeholder communities, and adult learning theory to develop a new suite of education and training materials for DCSA. The insights from the documentation and interviews provided us with the substantive information we needed for the materials and informed the preferred methods of delivery. Concurrently, we mapped the adult learning theories to each training material, ensuring that they adhered to the best possible learning techniques and practices for the SLTT LEA community and DCSA's particular role, authorities, and mission objectives. The eight types of materials we developed, located in Appendixes B through I, are as follows:

1. *CHRI Sharing Guidebook*: A comprehensive, baseline document that addresses each facet of CHRI sharing that SLTT LEAs would need to know, or be expected to know, to effectively and efficiently partner with DCSA for the purposes of CHRI sharing (and background investigations generally) (Appendix B).
2. *Frequently asked questions*: Provides information in a question-and-answer format according to the most frequently reported issues and questions that SLTT LEA personnel have regarding DCSA (and its organization, mission, and authorities) and common CHRI sharing impediments and solutions (Appendix C).
3. *Fact sheet*: A concise summary of critical DCSA and CHRI sharing points designed for meetings and conversations that DCSA personnel have with SLTT LEA personnel in various situations (e.g., introductions, in-person inquiries, training seminars, or conferences) (Appendix D).
4. *One-pagers* (three versions): Very brief distillations of DCSA, its authorities, and CHRI sharing procedures designed for rapid distribution and explanation in circumstances in which time is very limited (e.g., in-person law check or email/fax contact) (Appendix E).
5. *Brochures* (two styles): Short informational document designed to cover all major points from the training guidebook, but in a bullet-point and short-sentence style designed for broad distribution and/or leave-behind situations (Appendix F).
6. *Email*: Brief introduction of DCSA to SLTT LEA personnel or point of contact (POC); provides overview of DCSA and available education and training materials (Appendix G).
7. *Training presentation*: Reformulated version of DCSA's current training presentations designed to be more digestible for a broader SLTT LEA audience and shortened for interactions with SLTT LEAs that are time limited (Appendix H).
8. *Posters* (five versions): Visual distillations of DCSA's authorities, inquiry forms, and CHRI sharing procedures designed for distribution and public display at SLTT LEAs or law enforcement conferences and events to socialize and reinforce key CHRI sharing points (Appendix I).

Drafting and Revision of the Final Education and Training Materials: Pilot Field Testing

After developing an initial draft of the education and training materials, we sought stakeholder input from DCSA and potential end-users at SLTT LEAs via field testing. We contacted participants from SLTT LEAs and DCSA field offices who, during the interview phase, had previously shared their insights on the process and interactions of collecting CHRI. We then provided the complete suite of draft materials in electronic PDF format to these SLTT LEAs and DCSA offices.[1] Our POCs for the field testing distributed the materials to the appropriate end-users for their review and evaluation.

To collect feedback from their review and evaluation, POCs and end-users were provided with an information collection form to complete. This form, shown in Figure 5.1, was designed to ensure a standardized manner of data and information collection that could be used by both DCSA and SLTT LEA participants. Although compressed for size in this report, the form was sent in a Microsoft Word format that had sufficient space for participants to include as much or as little feedback as they believed was necessary to answer each survey question.

Four DCSA and four SLTT LEA jurisdictions provided feedback on the draft education and training materials. We combined the comments into an adjudication matrix used by the research and design team to assess all comments received and to record revisions made to the materials in response. Some of the feedback required purely cosmetic or otherwise nonsubstantive changes, such as the correction of minor inconsistencies in the application of phrases and terms across the various materials. For example, some end-users noted that the definition of CHRI (in materials that included this definition) should be consistent when referencing records of interactions with law enforcement that do not result in a criminal disposition. Thus, we standardized this phrasing across the products, i.e., "DCSA may also require additional information regarding other activities that do not result in criminal records." Other comments necessitated more substantive changes to improve the products. For example, DCSA end-user feedback noted that DCSA investigators are not, in fact, required to provide the subject waiver forms to SLTT LEAs when requesting CHRI, but that they "may" provide these forms upon request to SLTT LEAs.[2] We made this correction in all the materials where applicable.

Several comments supported the decisions made during development of the education and training materials or were particularly relevant to the overall messaging and efficacy of the materials. Many quotations, as shown in Table 5.1, helped reinforce the topics, subject matter, items for inclusion, and the formats selected for each of the education and training materials. For example, the Aaron Alexis matter was included in several materials to illustrate to SLTT LEA personnel what can happen when there is a breakdown in CHRI collection, collaboration, and sharing. The materials were formatted to be concise in response to repeated suggestions from stakeholders during our initial round of interviews and during the field testing that each product meet its educational and training objectives without extraneous verbiage or graphics. The comments received also pointed to images, wording, or formatting that needed to be changed to best convey the message of DCSA.

---

[1] For field testing, we enlisted the participation of four SLTT jurisdictions and four DCSA Field Offices. We were limited in the number of respondents that we could enlist by Office of Management and Budget (OMB) Paperwork Reduction Act (PRA) regulations (Code of Federal Regulations, Title 48, Section 1.106, OMB approval under the Paperwork Reduction Act) that specifically limit data and information collection efforts by federal agencies (and their contractors). Such collection efforts from entities (or persons, if the unit of analysis is individual persons) that exceed ten in number may be conducted but must be reviewed by, and must obtain approval from, OMB. Applying for OMB approval was not within the scope of this project. Additionally, we were limited to SLTT and DCSA offices that volunteered to make themselves available for this data collection, as neither group could be required to participate in the study.

[2] Clarification of the rule that DCSA investigators are not required to provide subject waiver forms to SLTT LEAs, but may do so upon request, was also provided by reference to the OPM's *Investigator Handbook*, 2007.

FIGURE 5.1
Field Testing Feedback Collection Form

DCSA CHRI Sharing Training Material/Tool Review Sheet	
Reviewer Name:	
Reviewer Field Office/Location:	
	Please describe your impressions of the training material/tool: positives, negatives, suggestions, or recommendations for improvement
Training Briefing	
Fact Sheet	
Posters (5 versions)	
	➢ Is there a poster that communicates the information best? If so, why?
One Pagers (3 versions)	
	➢ Is there a One Pager that communicates the information best? If so, why?
FAQs	
Guidebook	
Brochures (2 versions)	
	➢ Is there a brochure that communicates the information best? If so, why?
E-mail Introduction	
For all training materials/tools:	
Do you have general recommendations for improving the training materials/tools?	
How and under what kinds of circumstances would you or your staff use these materials/tools?	
Is there any pertinent information missing from the training materials/tools?	

Aaron Alexis: A breakdown in CHRI collection, collaboration, and sharing

On September 16, 2013, Aaron Alexis fatally shot 12 people and injured four others, including a police officer, at the headquarters of the Naval Sea Systems Command inside the Washington Navy Yard in Washington, D.C. Alexis served in the Navy for nearly four years from 2007 to 2011. Prior to and during this period, he was cited for misconduct at least eight times and arrested twice. None of his arrests led to prosecution. He was honorably discharged from the Navy and eligible to reenlist. Alexis received a Secret-level clearance in March 2008 after an investigation conducted by an OPM contractor. Alexis was arrested in Seattle, Washington, in 2004 for malicious mischief but never charged because of mishandled paperwork.

When applying for his clearance, Alexis neglected to mention the arrest because there was no conviction. The investigator, however, was able to uncover the incident from both the FBI database and a local law check. The local law check used the Washington Statewide Database, which included only minimal information on Alexis's investigative file. Had the investigation uncovered the original arresting documents, a more thorough evaluation of Alexis might have resulted in the denial of the clearance.[a]

[a] See U.S. Department of Justice, U.S. Attorney's Office, District of Columbia, "U.S. Attorney's Office Closes Investigation Involving Fatal Shooting of Aaron Alexis No Charges to Be Filed Against Officers Who Responded to Mass Murders at Washington Navy Yard," press release, August 27, 2014.

TABLE 5.1
Exemplar Quotations from Pilot Field Testing

Participant Type	Quote
DCSA	"I love that the Alexis matter was included as a real-world example of the importance of PD cooperation. That really drills down why we need PD assistance."
	"The training briefing was very clear and concise. I believe it will be easy for law enforcement agencies to understand DCSA's history, mission, and purpose for requesting law enforcement records."
	"I don't see any LEA posting this information in their dept/office."
	"The wording "PLEASE DO YOUR BEST TO MEET TIMELINES!" is unclear. The deadlines of whom? CJAs often operate on their own timeline when providing the CHRI and those timelines don't always mirror the desired 'deadline' of the Investigator."
	"Access to CHRI is requested not only from CJAs where an individual has lived, worked, or attended school, but also from CJAs where it is expected that a record should exist. For example, an individual could have vacationed near a lake and was arrested for Boating While Intoxicated."
SLTT LEA	"The only thing I have to say is for your agency to ensure everyone in the departments you collaborate with have this informative information, so no questions go unanswered. Especially when new people take over. This is the first time I have seen any of this information."
	"For those that are processing the requests, we like to know that we're giving DCSA what they want. I noticed in some of the documents when describing CHRI, the word "interactions" is used, which is not clear. I was also surprised to see "alleged or suspected criminal activity of a subject" is part of their criminal history. I think this will bring up a lot of questions. If you are not charged with a crime, how is this part of your criminal history?"
	"I found this very useful. Some of the questions I had while reading other materials were answered when I read through these. One question we have a lot is if we should give police reports where a subject attempted suicide or had some other type of mental situation that required law enforcement to intervene. This may be a good place to respond to that."

SOURCE: RAND interviews.
NOTE: CJA = criminal justice agency; PD = police department.

Feedback on Particular Materials

We solicited feedback for all the draft training education and training materials but did not receive detailed feedback from all reviewers for all products. However, some of the feedback was helpful in understanding and revising particular products. When asked for preferences—i.e., which poster or one-pager was more informative or useful—many of the commenters did not indicate a preferred product.

In terms of the posters presented, two SLTT reviewers preferred poster 2, as did one SAC. Meanwhile, two SACs preferred poster 3. Layout-based comments were helpful, regardless of the reviewer. For example, one reviewer from the SAC sample noted that poster 3 was a cleaner layout, while one SLTT responded that they preferred poster 2 because it was easy to read. This reinforced our decision to provide DCSA with multiple versions, so that stakeholders can select among the materials those that best meet their needs.

For one-pagers, version 3 appeared to be the most preferred version where a comment was recorded. However, we received positive comments for all the one-pagers, with one respondent noting that "All [one-pagers are] equally informative. I like that you have different versions." Additionally, we received some stylistic inputs to improve products, such as the use of certain graphics and layouts and the value of clear and concise material.

We also provided multiple versions of a brochure for participants to review. Comments received revealed no preference among SLTT users; SACs tended to prefer the trifold version. The brevity and conciseness of the document appeared to be beneficial and convincing factors for the SACs and reinforced similar comments for other training materials.

Using the Training Materials

The intent of the education and training materials is to equip DCSA SACs, investigators, and other personnel with tools that they can use to educate and train SLTT LEAs on CHRI sharing; as an introduction to DCSA (both personally and institutionally); and as a leave-behind after a visit, meeting, seminar, or other interaction. These uses are also mapped to the content of each of the products, in that each product can be used for one or more purposes (e.g., describing DCSA as an organization, explaining the definition of CHRI, delineating DCSA authorities), or in one or more venues (e.g., short introductory meeting, seminar presentation, small group discussion). SLTT participants affirmatively noted they would use the materials to train their personnel, especially for new employees.

We also learned that, in some cases, additional context was needed to elaborate on or clarify the information contained in select materials. In certain examples, this feedback was critical to ensure that SLTT LEAs understood DCSA's broad information needs. One SLTT LEA user noted that "I was also surprised to see 'alleged or suspected criminal activity of a subject' is part of their criminal history. I think this will bring up a lot of questions. If you are not charged with a crime, how is this part of your criminal history?" Interestingly, this point was also brought up by a DCSA SAC, who recommended "that the documents make clear the importance of [criminal justice agencies] providing all, not just some, CHRI to Investigators." These comments prompted the research team to make changes to accommodate activities and contact with law enforcement that were not necessarily criminal but would be helpful for an investigator to know when conducting an investigation.

Revising the Training Materials

We edited and amended the education and training materials according to the feedback provided by participants in the pilot field testing. We adjudicated each editorial comment, suggestion, and recommendation individually to determine whether it warranted a change to the draft materials. Most changes were not substantive—i.e., they related to typos, term usage and phrasing, formatting, and other aesthetic issues. Some comments were more substantive in nature, and a change was made in these instances if it improved the substance, accuracy, clarity, and consistency of the materials (both internally across the materials themselves and externally with DCSA documents, authorities, processes, and practices). The final suite of education and training materials is contained in Appendixes B through I.

Conclusion

In summary, the RAND team designed and developed education and training materials to help DCSA meet the challenge of building CHRI sharing partnerships with SLTT LEAs to improve the agency's ability to conduct effective and efficient federal background investigations and personnel vetting. We developed these materials with two objectives in mind: (1) assess the current educational and training needs of SLTT LEAs, and (2) develop education and training materials to address current gaps related to CHRI reporting compliance by SLTTs. Our approach to meet these objectives focused on applying the prevailing learning theories to the relevant missions, data, information, and needs of both DCSA and the SLTT LEA organizations from which it collects CHRI. From this research, and particularly from interviews with DCSA and SLTT staff, we identified current gaps and impediments to training and developed specific education and training materials to overcome those impediments and gaps. Our suite of eight recommended materials is designed to help DCSA educate and train SLTT LEAs across all key learning objectives, venues, and circumstances to enable DCSA to build more robust CHRI sharing partnerships.

APPENDIX A

Methodology Framework

Tables A.1 through A.8 in this appendix describe the framework elements for each of the education and training materials, expanding on how the applicable learning theories were employed to develop the education and training materials themselves. For each type of material, we describe the applied learning theory, the learning objectives, the intended audience, the recommended topics covered, the messaging of these topics to the LEA audience, and the intended application (i.e., the use or method of deployment). Table A.9 describes which learning objectives (e.g., who is DCSA? what does the law require?) are addressed by education and training materials. As the table illustrates, many of the training materials achieve all the stated objectives, while others, such as the one-pagers and posters, were developed to specifically address a select subset—a deliberate approach that built flexibility into how the suite of materials could be used to achieve different goals.

TABLE A.1
Framework Elements for the Fact Sheet

	Fact Sheet
Learning theory	Experiential learning
Application	Used with the training module as a hands-on product that relates to the participants' experience
Learning objective	<ul><li>What should you do if DCSA contacts you?</li><li>Who is DCSA?</li><li>What does DCSA do, and how does it relate to national security?</li><li>What is DCSA interested in?</li><li>What authorities does DCSA have?</li><li>What are forms and methods used by DCSA?</li></ul>
Audience for the training	SLTT/LEA
Recommended topics for training	What is a national security background check, and how is it different from other checks?
Recommended messaging to SLTT/LEA	<ul><li>Clearly state that the DCSA mission requires cooperation from SLTT LEAs<ul><li>DCSA can obtain state attorney general permissions and opinions; use examples of other SLTT LEAs that have helped meet DCSA missions.</li></ul></li><li>Start with *why*<ul><li>Connect CHRI sharing and national security</li><li>Stress employment purposes</li><li>Stress the waiver process and protections.</li></ul></li></ul>
Messaging included in tool	<ul><li>Introduction of what DCSA is and its mission</li><li>Examples of CHRI: actions an LEA can take when contacted by DCSA, how DCSA contacts LEAs, who will contact the agencies, and DCSA authorities</li><li>Full contact information included for Safety and Security, Liaison Office, and Records Outreach.</li></ul>
Intended application	Standalone information sheet, handout, or as a reference file (print and/or PDF). Similar to the one-pager but in a modified format with more text, background, and thorough contact information.

TABLE A.2
Framework Elements for Frequently Asked Questions

	Frequently Asked Questions
Learning theory	Andragogy
Application	Supplemental training material enhanced by adult learning principles such as explanation of purpose, increase of motivation, and readiness to learn
Learning objective	• Who is DCSA? • What does DCSA do, and how does it relate to national security? • What is DCSA interested in? • What authorities does DCSA have? • What does the law require? • What are forms and methods used by DCSA?
Audience for the training	SLTT/LEA
Recommended topics for training	• What is a national security background check, and how is it different from other checks? • DCSA authorities

Recommended messaging to SLTT/LEA	• Clearly state the DCSA mission requires cooperation from SLTT LEAs
	   – DCSA can obtain state attorney general permissions and opinions; use examples of other SLTT LEAs that have helped meet DCSA missions
	• Start with *why*
	   – Connect CHRI sharing and national security
	   – Stress employment purposes
	   – Stress the waiver process and protections.

Messaging included in tool	The information given is intended to encompass the entirety of questions that may arise related to training topics of interest.
Intended application	Standalone information packet, handout, or as a reference file (print and/or PDF); may substitute or supplement the other training materials, depending on needs of LEA.

TABLE A.3
Framework Elements for the Training Briefing

	Training Briefing for Law Enforcement Agencies
Learning theory	Experiential learning
Application	Used as a training module as a hands-on product that relates to the participants' experience
Learning objective	• Who is DCSA? • What does DCSA do, and how does it relate to national security? • What is DCSA interested in? • What authorities does DCSA have? • What does the law require? • What should you do if DCSA contacts you?
Audience for the training	SLTT/LEA

Recommended messaging to SLTT/LEA	• Clearly state that the DCSA mission requires cooperation from SLTT LEAs
	   – DCSA can obtain state attorney general permissions and opinions; use examples of other SLTT LEAs that have helped meet DCSA missions.
	• Start with *why*
	   – Connect CHRI sharing and national security
	   – Stress employment purposes
	   – Stress the waiver process and protections.

Messaging included in tool	The information is intended to give a detailed overview of DCSA, its people, mission, needs, authorities, and interactions with LEAs.
Intended application	This briefing can be given in person or virtually to groups of LEAs. Audiences include records personnel, leadership, and others interested or involved in CHRI sharing.

TABLE A.4
Framework Elements for Posters

	Posters				
	Poster 1	Poster 2	Poster 3	Poster 4	Poster 5
Learning theory	Self-directed				
Application	Used as a reminder or reference				
Learning objective	What are the forms and methods used by DCSA?	What should you do if DCSA contacts you?	What should you do if DCSA contacts you?	What are the forms and methods of communication used by DCSA?	What should you do if DCSA contacts you?
Audience for the training	SLTT/LEA				
Recommended topics for training	Explain forms used to collect information	State process used by DCSA to collect CHRI	Explain the role of LEAs in the DCSA CHRI collection process	Explain forms used to collect information	State process used by DCSA to collect CHRI
Recommended messaging to SLTT/LEA	Description and explanation of INV Form 44; contact information for additional questions	Description of how LEAs could support DCSA in collecting CHRI, contact information, and reminder about timelines	Description of how LEAs could support DCSA in collecting CHRI, contact information, and reminder about timelines	Description and an example of how DCSA could contact an agency and request CHRI for a subject	Basic description of what steps to take if DCSA contacts an LEA; includes contact information
Messaging	Quick reference				

TABLE A.5
Framework Elements for Brochures

	Brochure(s)	
	Brochure 7 x 9	Brochure Trifold
Learning theory	Self-directed	
Application	Used as a pre-training handout or additional reference	
Learning objective	<ul><li>Who is DCSA?</li><li>What does DCSA do, and how does it relate to national security?</li><li>What authorities does DCSA have?</li><li>What does the law require?</li><li>What forms and methods are used in DCSA?</li><li>What should you do if DCSA contacts you?</li></ul>	
Audience for the training	SLTT/LEA	
Recommended messaging to SLTT/LEA	<ul><li>Clearly state that the DCSA mission requires cooperation from SLTT LEAs.</li><li>Start with *why*<ul><li>Connect CHRI sharing and national security</li><li>Stress employment purposes</li><li>Stress the waiver process and protections.</li></ul></li></ul>	
Messaging included in tool	<ul><li>Who DCSA and contractor personnel are</li><li>DCSA's needs</li><li>The why (national security and authorization to collect)</li><li>Definition of CHRI authorities; full contact information is included</li></ul>	
Intended application	Standalone information sheet, marketing material, or as a reference file (print and/or PDF)	

TABLE A.6
Framework Elements for Email

	Email
Learning theory	Not applicable
Application	Used to make contact with LEAs in a uniform fashion
Learning objective	• Who is DCSA? • What does DCSA do, and how does it relate to national security? • What is DCSA interested in? • What training opportunities are available?
Audience for the training	SLTT/LEA
Recommended topics for training	• Brief outline of DCSA needs and mission • Information about the materials and training that are available
Recommended messaging to SLTT/LEA	• Brief outline of DCSA needs and mission • Information about the materials and training that are available
Messaging	Email outreach

TABLE A.7
Framework Elements for One-Pagers

	One-Pager(s)		
	One-Pager 1	One-Pager 2	One-Pager 3
Learning theory	Self-directed		
Application	Use as a pre-training handout and/or introduce need for training by focusing on self-assessment		
Learning objective	• Who is DCSA? • What does DCSA do, and how does it relate to national security? • What is DCSA interested in?		
Audience for the training	SLTT/LEA		
Recommended topics for training	All (DCSA history; CHRI sharing process with DCSA; timing and deadlines for CHRI requests; reference guides for what types of information DCSA needs; what a national security background check is and how it is different from other checks; DCSA authorities; what can be expected from a DCSA investigator or contractor; DCSA chains of command)		

Recommended messaging to SLTT/LEA	• Start with *why*
	  – Connect CHRI sharing and national security
	  – Stress employment purposes.
	• Stress the waiver process and protections
	• Clearly state that the DCSA mission requires cooperation from SLTT LEAs and that DCSA can obtain state attorney general permissions and opinions
	• Use examples of other SLTT LEAs that have helped meet DCSA missions		

Messaging	• Explanation of who the personnel are, what the needs of the agency and contractors are, importance of sharing information • Definitions of CHRI	• Explanation of what DCSA is, what it does, and what it needs • Definition of CHRI and why it is needed • Reverse side includes information on why it is important to share CHRI and detailed contact information	• Who DCSA and contractor personnel are • DCSA's needs • The *why* (national security and authorization to collect) • Definition of CHRI
Intended application	Standalone information sheet, handout, or as a reference file (print and/or PDF)		

TABLE A.8
Framework Elements for Guidebook

	Guidebook
Learning theory	Self-directed
Application	Used as a reference guide
Learning objective	• Who is DCSA? • What does DCSA do, and how does it relate to national security? • What is DCSA interested in? • What authorities does DCSA have? • What does the law require? • What are forms and methods used by DCSA? • What should you do if DCSA contacts you?
Audience for the training	SLTT/LEA
Recommended messaging to SLTT/LEA	Provides a comprehensive overview to the DCSA mission and CHRI sharing

Messaging included in tool	• The guidebook is arranged in the following order:
	  – Who is DCSA?
	  – What are DCSA's authorities?
	  – How do DCSA staff members perform their duties?
	  – What information is DCSA authorized to collect?

Intended application	Reference file (print and/or PDF), used to guide and supplement trainings from DCSA or LEA

TABLE A.9
Mapping Learning Objectives to DCSA Training Materials

Materials	Objectives						
	Who is DCSA?	What does DCSA do, and how does it relate to national security?	What is DCSA interested in, i.e., types of CHRI?	What authorities does DCSA have?	What does the law require?	What should you do if DCSA contacts you?	What are forms or methods used by DCSA?
One-pager 1	X	X	X				
One-pager 2	X	X	X				
One-pager 3	X	X	X				
Fact sheet	X	X	X	X	X	X	X
FAQ	X	X	X	X	X	X	X
Poster 1							X
Poster 2						X	
Poster 3						X	
Poster 4							X
Poster 5						X	
Guidebook	X	X	X	X	X	X	X
Brochure 7 x 9	X	X	X	X	X	X	X
Brochure trifold	X	X	X	X	X	X	X
Email	X	X	X				
Training briefing	X	X	X	X	X	X	X

APPENDIX B

CHRI Sharing Guidebook

The *CHRI Sharing Guidebook* is designed to be a comprehensive, baseline document that anchors DCSA's educational and training materials. The Guidebook addresses each facet of CHRI sharing that SLTT LEAs would need to know or be expected to know to effectively and efficiently partner with DCSA for the purposes of CHRI sharing:

- DCSA as an organization
- DCSA authorities
- CHRI collection processes and procedures
- what constitutes CHRI
- how CHRI sharing can be made easier.

As a foundational document, the Guidebook will provide DCSA with the ability to fully inform SLTT LEAs and any other stakeholders should any of these entities request or require detailed information and instructions.

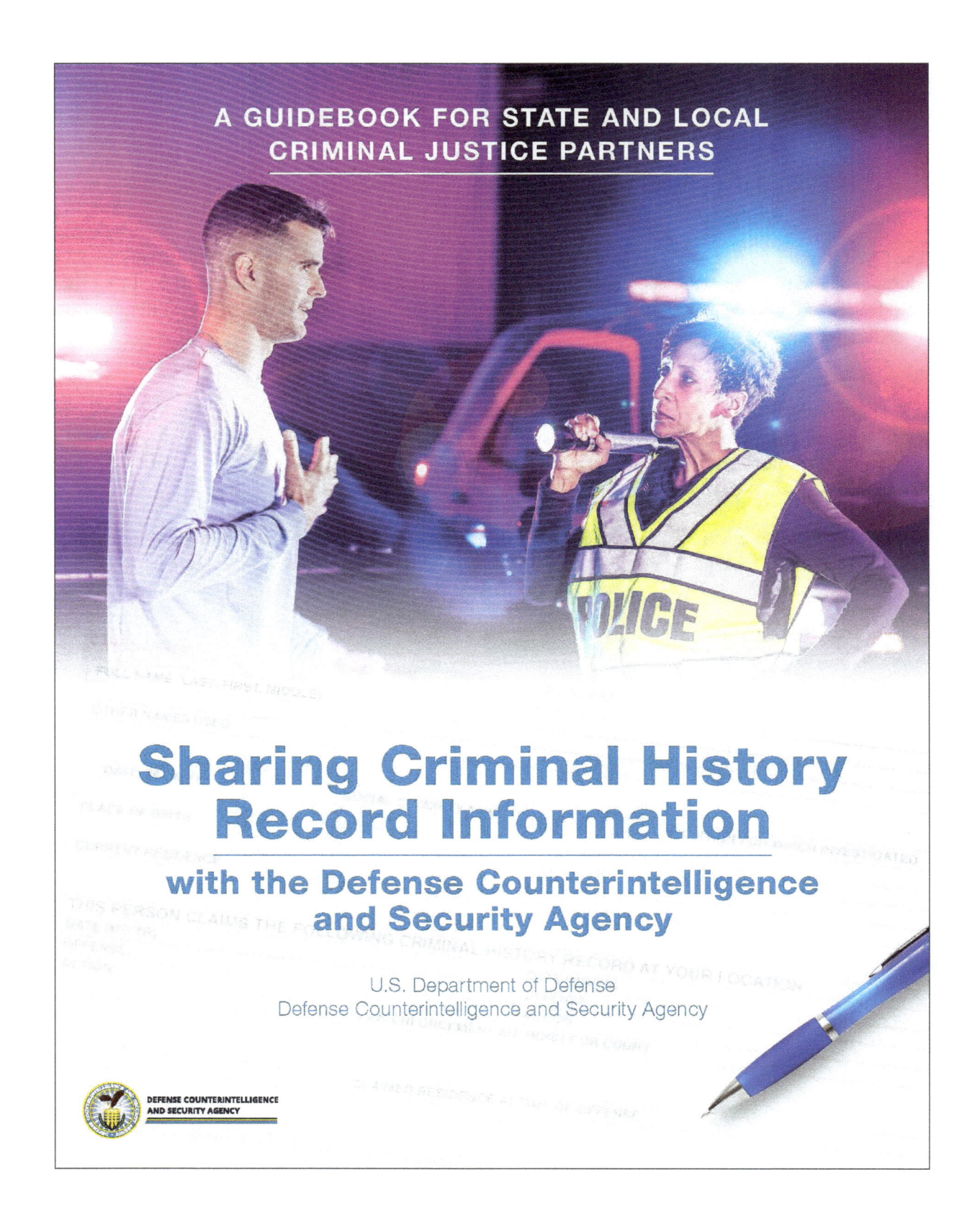

A GUIDEBOOK FOR STATE AND LOCAL CRIMINAL JUSTICE PARTNERS

Sharing Criminal History Record Information
with the Defense Counterintelligence and Security Agency

U.S. Department of Defense
Defense Counterintelligence and Security Agency

A GUIDEBOOK FOR STATE AND LOCAL CRIMINAL JUSTICE PARTNERS

Sharing Criminal History Record Information

with the Defense Counterintelligence and Security Agency

U.S. Department of Defense
Defense Counterintelligence and Security Agency

Distribution: All U.S. state, local, tribal, and territorial jurisdictions
Prepared by DCSA, Law Enforcement Liaison Office, April 2022

DEFENSE COUNTERINTELLIGENCE AND SECURITY AGENCY

1. PURPOSE: This guidebook provides state, local, tribal, and territorial (SLTT) criminal justice agency partners with detailed information on how to share criminal history record information (CHRI) efficiently and effectively with the U.S. Department of Defense, Defense Counterintelligence and Security Agency (DCSA). The information in this guidebook will facilitate knowledge development and partnership building with all criminal justice agencies across the nation.

Sharing CHRI with DCSA is a requirement for all criminal justice agencies pursuant to Title 5 of the U.S. Code, Section 9101. It is also a vital component to ensuring the trustworthiness and integrity of the U.S. government's federal and military workforce and an essential element of protecting and preserving national security and public safety. The information in this guidebook is designed to inform and educate SLTT criminal justice agency leaders, managers, and staff at all levels about DCSA as an organization, its missions, its authorities, and processes and procedures for CHRI sharing.

2. APPLICABILITY: This guidebook applies to all SLTT criminal justice agencies in the United States, including (but not limited to) the following:

a. law enforcement agencies (e.g., police departments, sheriffs' departments, campus police) with Originating Agency Identification (ORI) numbers having 0 through 9 as a ninth character

b. pre-trial service and release agencies (ORIs ending in "B")

c. correctional institutions (ORIs ending in "C")

d. custodial facilities (ORIs ending in "M")

e. probation and parole agencies (ORIs ending in "G")

f. courts and magistrates (ORIs ending in "J")

g. other agencies classified as criminal justice agencies (ORIs ending in "Y").

3. REFERENCE: DCSA Guidebook, *Sharing Criminal History Record Information with the Defense Counterintelligence and Security Agency*, Version 1.0, 2022.

4. CONTACT: Questions concerning this guidebook should be addressed to the DCSA Law Enforcement Liaison Office (LELO) at: (202) 606-1606, DCSA.Law-Enforcement-Liaison@mail.mil, or the following address:

U.S. Department of Defense

Defense Counterintelligence and Security Agency

Attn: Law Enforcement Liaison Office

1900 E Street, NW

Washington, DC 20415

BY ORDER OF THE DIRECTOR OF THE DCSA

DEFENSE COUNTERINTELLIGENCE AND SECURITY AGENCY

Contents

Chapter One. Who Is DCSA? 1

Chapter Two. Why Is Sharing CHRI with DCSA Important? 7

Chapter Three. What Are DCSA's Authorities? 9

Chapter Four. What Information Is DCSA Authorized to Collect? 12

Chapter Five. How Do DCSA Staff Perform Their Duties? 14

Chapter Six. How Can CHRI Sharing with DCSA Be Made Easier? 17

Appendix A. DCSA Statutory and Executive Order Authorities 23

Appendix B. Data Collection Forms..25

Appendix C. U.S. Department of Justice Letter to State and
Local Law Enforcement Agencies and Courts 27

Appendix D. DCSA Organization Nationwide 30

Appendix E. DCSA Contact Information..31

Abbreviations 31

Endnotes 32

References 35

Criminal History Record Information Sharing with the Defense Counterintelligence and Security Agency

Chapter One
Who Is DCSA?

A Brief History of DCSA

In 1953, the Civil Service Commission (CSC) received the authority to operate and manage the federal government's civilian personnel security program, which included conducting background investigations for sensitive positions. The power to perform background investigations for federal employees remained with the CSC until the formation of the Office of Personnel Management (OPM) in 1978 when the new agency assumed responsibility for non–Department of Defense (DoD) investigations. CSC and, subsequently, OPM represented one of two main investigative programs within the federal government.

In January 1972, the Defense Investigative Service (DIS) was established to conduct personnel security for DoD, creating the second largest vetting program within the federal government. The Defense Investigative Service carried out that mission for 33 years, which included a name change in 1997 to the Defense Security Service.[1] In February 2005, DoD's personnel security investigation mission transferred to OPM, making OPM the largest personnel security investigation provider in the federal government.

In 2016, the semiautonomous National Background Investigations Bureau (NBIB) was established under OPM to continue personnel vetting for the federal government. In April 2019, the president transferred the background investigative mission back to DoD and the Defense Security Service through Executive Order 13869 (see full timeline in Figure 1).[2] In anticipation of the transfer, DoD renamed its Defense Security Service the Defense Counterintelligence and Security Agency (DCSA) in June 2019. In October 2019, NBIB and the federal background investigative mission officially transferred from OPM to DoD, making DCSA the largest security agency in the federal government.[3]

Figure 1. Federal Background Investigative Function Timeline

January 1, 1972 — Defense Investigative Service established under DoD

1997 — Reorganization of DIS into Defense Security Service (DSS)

2005 — DSS investigative services function transferred to OPM

2016 — Semiautonomous NBIB established under OPM

2019 — Executive Order directed the transfer of NBIB to DSS and the renaming of DSS to DCSA

Mission

With the transfer of the investigative mission and NBIB to DCSA, the agency now conducts 95 percent of the federal government's background investigations. DCSA services over 100 federal entities, oversees 10,000 cleared companies, and conducts over 2.5 million background investigations each year.[4] It is the nation's primary investigative service provider of effective, efficient, and secure background investigations for the federal government. DCSA also carries out responsibilities for supervising industrial security, performing security education and training, and supporting counterintelligence activities.[5] DCSA's mission is as follows:

> Through vetting, industry engagement, counterintelligence support, and education, secure the trustworthiness of the United States Government's workforce, the integrity of its cleared contractor support, and the uncompromised nature of its technologies, services, and supply chains.[6]

DCSA fulfills its personnel security mission by conducting background investigations on civilian and military applicants, federal employees, employees of government contractors, and consultants to federal programs. The agency employs a network of investigators who work around the globe to carry out this mission. Background investigations are conducted to determine

- suitability for government employment
- fitness for appointment to an excepted service position
- fitness to perform work under a government contract
- eligibility to serve in a national security–sensitive position
- acceptance or retention in the armed forces

- eligibility for access to classified information
- eligibility for logical or physical access to a federally controlled facility or information technology system.[7]

The scope of a background investigation varies depending on the sensitivity of the position for which an individual applies. To be able to accurately adjudicate background investigations, it is vital that DCSA have access to criminal history record information (CHRI) from the criminal justice agencies with jurisdiction where an individual has lived, worked, or attended school and/or a location where a subject has admitted to a violation of law during the investigative period. DCSA typically requests this information from state, local, tribal, and territorial (SLTT) criminal justice agencies.[8]

DCSA also runs checks with federal agencies, including a fingerprint search with the Federal Bureau of Investigation (FBI), as part of background investigations. Some investigations may also involve checks of credit history and military service records, as well as interviews with the subject and neighbors, employers, personal references, and others with relevant knowledge of the individual. This information helps DCSA determine whether federal government employees and applicants are trustworthy, reliable, of good conduct and character, and have complete and unswerving loyalty to the United States.[9]

Organization of DCSA

DCSA's organizational structure features multiple functional directorates, divisions, and programs to support its various missions: Background Investigations (BI), Adjudications (ADJ), Vetting Risk Operations (VRO), National Background Investigative Service (NBIS), Critical Technology Protection (CTP), Counterintelligence (CI), DoD Insider Threat Management and Analysis Center (DITMAC), and Security Training (Figure 2).[10] SLTT criminal justice agencies interact with DCSA primarily through its BI division. BI manages part of the personnel vetting mission, conducting background investigations for federal government agencies and the U.S. military.[11] The Assistant Director of the Background Investigations directorate serves as the functional chief for background investigations and reports directly to DCSA's director.[12]

The Background Investigations Directorate

The Assistant Director of the Background Investigations Directorate oversees four supporting programs: Field Operations, Federal Investigative Records Enterprise (FIRE), Quality Oversight, and Customer and Stakeholder Engagement (Figure 3). Law enforcement agencies primarily interact with representatives from Field Operations, but they may also encounter individuals from FIRE and Customer and Stakeholder Engagement. The Field Operations program oversees DCSA's investigator staff. Field Operations has 58 field offices across three regions (northern, western, and central) of the United States (see Appendix D).[13] Field Operations investigators conduct investigative

Figure 2. DCSA Organizational Chart

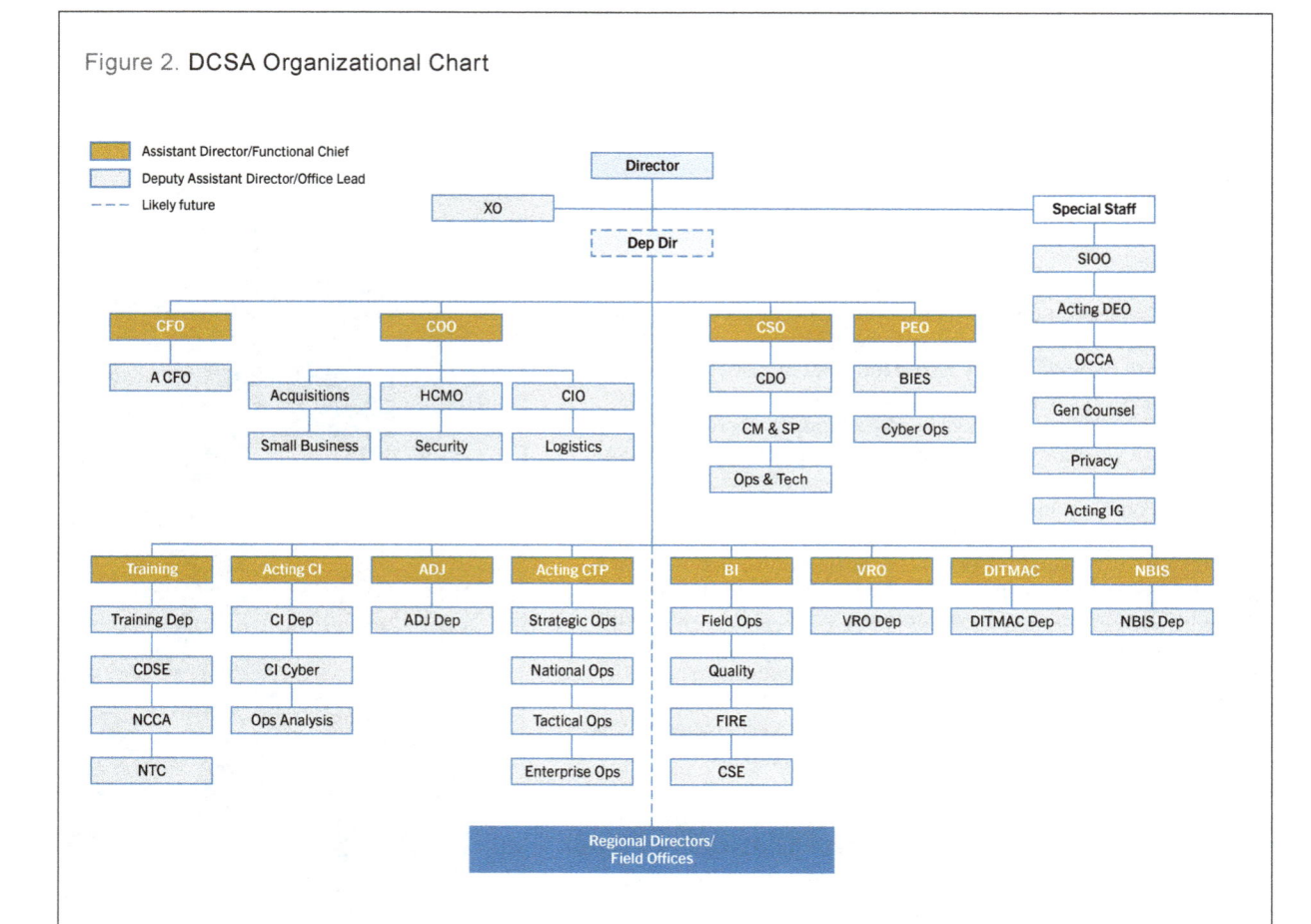

SOURCE: Derived from Lietzau, 2021.
NOTE: A CFO = Assistant Chief Financial Officer; BIES = Background Investigations Enterprise Systems; CDO = Chief Data Officer; CDSE = Center for Development of Security Excellence; CFO = Chief Financial Officer; CIO = Chief Information Officer; CM & SP = Change Management and Strategic Planning; COO = Chief Operating Officer; CSE = Customer and Stakeholder Engagements; CSO = Chief Strategy Officer; DEO = Diversity and Equal Opportunity; Dep = Deputy; Dir = Director; Gen = general; HCMO = Human Capital Management Office; IG = Inspector General; NCCA = National Center for Credibility Assessment; NTC = National Training Center; OCCA = Office of Communications and Congressional Affairs; Ops = operations; PEO = Program Executive Officer; SIOO = Senior Intelligence Oversight Official; Tech = technology; XO = Executive Officer.

checks and thus are the DCSA employees that law enforcement agencies interact with most frequently.

Special Agents-in-Charge manage investigators in the field and represent DCSA in their respective regions. They serve as the lead points of contact for any issues or challenges that may arise during the CHRI sharing process.[14] The FIRE program sends law enforcement agencies the initial investigative request forms discussed later in this manual.[15] Law enforcement agencies may need to contact FIRE's Records Outreach Office for questions about completing and submitting these forms to DCSA.[16] Finally, the Customer and Stakeholder Engagement program includes the Law Enforcement Liaison Office (LELO), which provides support to law enforcement agencies sharing CHRI with DCSA. LELO conducts research and analysis, identifies new sources of CHRI and other law-related data, and educates and provides technical support to stakeholder criminal justice and law enforcement agencies.[17]

DCSA Investigative Personnel

As stated previously, the Field Operations division engages in the field work necessary to complete background investigations, from in-person interviews with subjects and their contacts to collecting CHRI from various criminal justice and law enforcement agencies. DCSA investigators consist of two distinct groups: federal and contract investigators. As of the publication date of this Guidebook, DCSA directly employs around 1,500 federal investigators. DCSA also contracts with multiple private investigative companies to employ around 5,000 contract investigators.[18] Consequently, law enforcement agencies will likely encounter both federal and contractor personnel when they conduct investigative checks.

While federal investigators are federal employees, and contract investigators are employees of their respective private companies, federal law grants contract investigators the same authority to access CHRI as federal investigators.[19] Accordingly, they should be given the same information, no matter the color of their badge or their respective employers. DCSA contracts with multiple private investigative companies at any

Figure 3. DCSA Background Investigations Directorate

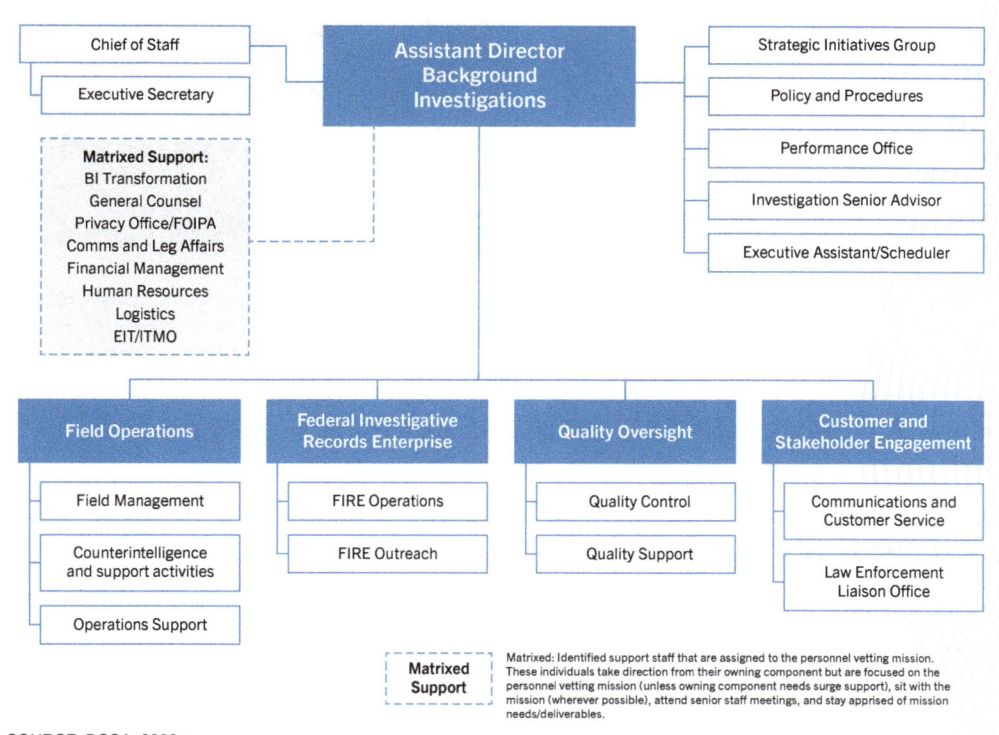

SOURCE: DCSA, 2020a.
NOTE: Comms = communications; EIT = electronic and information technology; FOIPA = Freedom of Information and Privacy Acts; ITMO = Information Technology Management Office; Leg = legislative.

given time. Therefore, law enforcement agencies may come across different investigative company names as they encounter investigators over time. For example, as of 2021, DCSA contracted with companies such as Securitas, CACI, and Prospecta to perform some of the investigative functions.[20]

Chapter Two
Why Is Sharing CHRI with DCSA Important?

It is imperative that DCSA receive CHRI from SLTT criminal justice agencies to mitigate insider threats. *Insiders* are individuals with legitimate, authorized access to an organization's personnel, facilities, information, equipment, networks, and systems. The threat comes from the potential for an insider to use their legitimate access to cause harm to an organization or the nation. This harm can be malicious or unintentional and could come in many forms: spying, terrorism, unauthorized release of information, corruption, sabotage, workplace violence, or others.[21]

Reviewing CHRI as part of an individual's background investigation is one way in which DCSA tries to mitigate insider threats. While individuals are required to tell the truth about their background under penalty of law, that information must be verified. CHRI, even from agencies in areas where an individual may no longer reside, helps determine whether an individual failed to report information and should be placed in a position of public trust. A DCSA investigator will request all CHRI on an individual, including information about any local felonies, misdemeanors, traffic offenses, or other law violations regardless of whether they resulted in a conviction. Investigators will need pertinent information about each offense, including its date and location, charg-

| 7 |

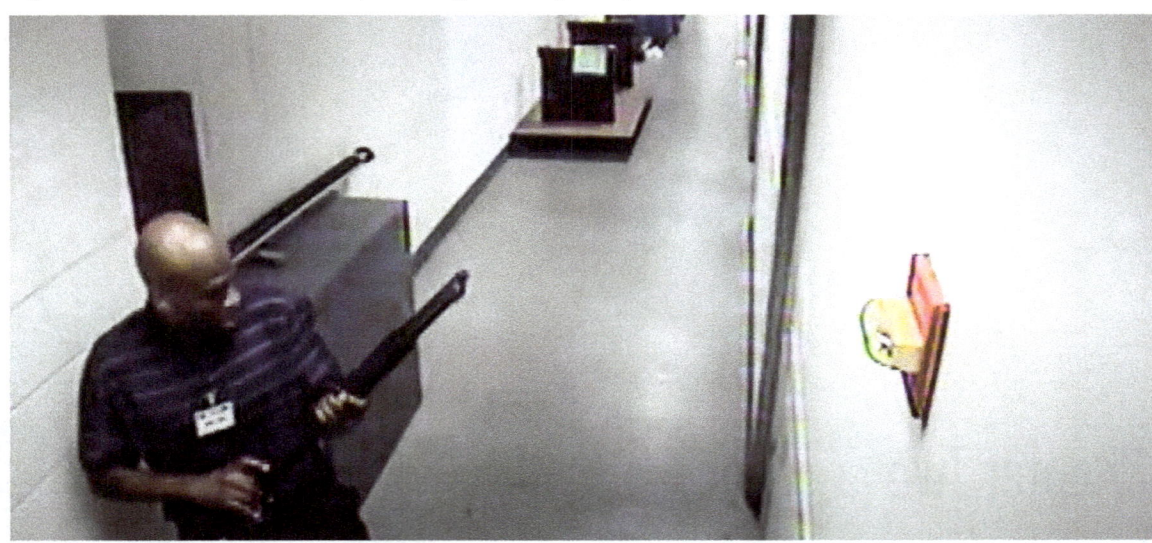

Figure 4. Assailant Aaron Alexis, Washington Navy Yard, 2012

SOURCE: FBI.

ing statements, circumstances related to the offense, and dispositions. Investigators may also ask for a copy of police reports; these reports may be requested of any alleged or suspected criminal activity, regardless of whether the activity led to an arrest, charge, or conviction.[22]

What can happen when incomplete CHRI is provided? On September 16, 2013, Aaron Alexis fatally shot 12 people and injured four others, including a police officer, at the headquarters of the Naval Sea Systems Command inside the Washington Navy Yard in Washington, D.C. (Figure 4).[23] Alexis served in the Navy for nearly four years from 2007 to 2011. He was cited for misconduct at least eight times and arrested twice. None of his arrests led to prosecution. He was honorably discharged from the Navy and eligible to reenlist. Alexis received a Secret-level clearance in March 2008 after an investigation conducted by an OPM contractor. Alexis was arrested in Seattle, Washington in 2004 for malicious mischief but never charged because of mishandled paperwork.

When applying for his clearance, Alexis neglected to mention the arrest because there was no conviction. The investigator, however, was able to uncover the incident from both the FBI database and a local law check. The local law check used the Washington Statewide Database, which included only minimal information on Alexis's investigative file. Had the investigator taken additional steps to get access to the original arresting documents, that person might have seen more details leading to Alexis's arrest and statements by his father suggesting that he had posttraumatic stress disorder. This additional information could have led to an order for a mental evaluation of Alexis prior to the final adjudication of his clearance application. Further, the investigator later interviewed Alexis. Without law enforcement records of his 2004 arrest, however, the investigator was not able to get a full account of the incident, including the use of a weapon or emotional state at the time, which would have informed adjudication.[24]

Chapter Three
What Are DCSA's Authorities?

Many SLTT criminal justice and law enforcement departments and agencies are unaware of DCSA's authority and, as a result, may question whether they should provide very detailed information to DCSA investigators. A series of federal laws, executive orders, and regulations authorize and empower DCSA to collect CHRI from SLTT departments and agencies. Because the primary federal statute that grants DCSA its authority supersedes (i.e., preempts) any and all state laws, SLTT departments and agencies are required to respond to DCSA requests for CHRI and provide any records and/or information responsive to the request.[25] Additionally, based on how the law defines CHRI, DCSA's legal authority grants the agency broader access to CHRI than that of public, commercial, or other entities seeking CHRI for employment purposes.

More specifically, federal statutory law 5 U.S.C. 9101 ("Access to criminal history records for national security and other purposes") section (b)(1) requires SLTTs to provide DCSA with all requested CHRI (or provide access to the CHRI) in accordance with the Federal Investigative Standards.[26] Federal law also provides that criminal justice and law enforcement agencies are not legally liable for any information given to DCSA for the purpose of background investigations.[27] Thus, so long as SLTT departments and agencies comply with the elements of 5 U.S.C. 9101 requiring them to share information with DCSA, subjects may not claim that their CHRI was improperly disclosed.

| 9 |

The law defines CHRI broadly as follows:

> Information collected by criminal justice agencies on individuals consisting of identifiable descriptions and notations of arrests, indictments, information(s), or other formal criminal charges, and any disposition arising therefrom, sentencing, correction supervision, and release. The term does not include identification information such as fingerprint records to the extent that such information does not indicate involvement of the individual in the criminal justice system. The term includes those records of a state or locality sealed pursuant to law if such records are accessible by State and local criminal justice agencies for the purpose of conducting background checks.[28]

In addition, 5 U.S.C. 9101 explains that the purpose of a DCSA background investigation is to ensure that individuals under investigation for a security clearance are, in fact, eligible for federal employment in a sensitive position, meet the basic suitability or fitness requirements for federal or contract employment, or meet the suitability requirements for a public trust position or accession or retention in the armed forces and/or identity credentialing under Homeland Security Presidential Directive 12 (HSPD-12).[29] Other applicable authorities are as follows:

- Pursuant to and consistent with section 3001(c) of the Intelligence Reform and Terrorism Prevention Act of 2004 (50 U.S.C. 3341(c)),[30]

| 10 |

sections 925(a)(1) and (d)(2) of the National Defense Authorization Act for Fiscal Year 2018 (10 U.S.C. 1564 note),[31] and Executive Order 13467, 2008,[32] DCSA is designated as "the primary entity for conducting effective, efficient, and secure background investigations for the federal government."
- Executive Order 13467: Reforming Processes Related to Suitability for Government Employment, Fitness for Contractor Employees, and Eligibility for Access to Classified National Security Information (June 30, 2008), as amended. This executive order was extensively amended by Executive Order 13869, Transferring Responsibilities for Background Investigations to the DoD, on April 24, 2019.[33]
- Title 5, Code of Federal Regulations, Part 731, regarding the adjudication of suitability and fitness determinations for federal personnel and contractors.[34]

To facilitate further understanding of the above authorities, the U.S. Department of Justice issued an open letter to all SLTT criminal justice and law enforcement agencies and courts to emphasize the importance of CHRI sharing with the U.S. government for the purposes of background investigation (see Appendix C). This letter was issued shortly after the Washington Navy Yard shooting by a former Navy service member and U.S. government contractor, Aaron Alexis (see discussion in Chapter Two).

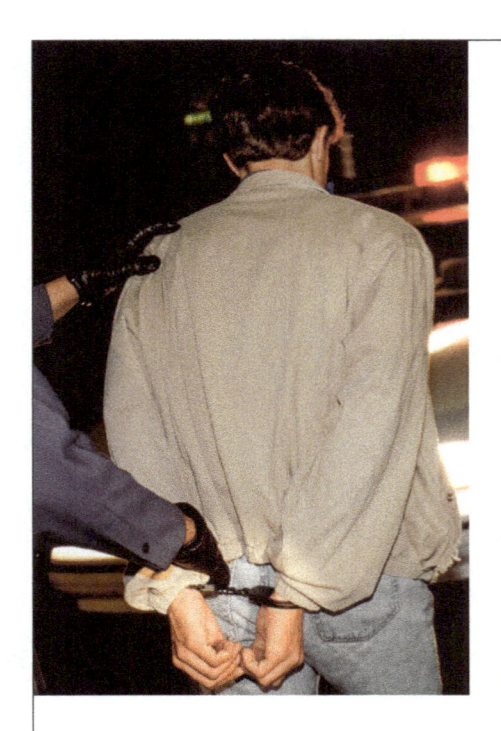

Chapter Four
What Information Is DCSA Authorized to Collect?

As described in Chapter Two, DCSA's authority to collect CHRI is extremely broad and covers all aspects of criminal activity that a subject may have engaged in or may have been suspected of engaging in, regardless of whether there has been an arrest or court disposition. DCSA may also require additional information regarding other activities that do not result in criminal records.

DCSA's collection authority is not limited by law to public-only available CHRI in the manner that most public, commercial, or private entities are restricted. DCSA's access and collection authority is equivalent to that of any federal or SLTT law enforcement or criminal justice agency engaged in the background investigations and vetting of its own personnel. Pursuant to this expansive authority, the categories of criminal activity that a subject may engage in, and that should be shared with DCSA, include the following:[35]

- felonies
- misdemeanors
- juvenile offenses
- traffic offenses
- any other violations of criminal laws, whether they resulted in a conviction or not.

Under the law, any records or information that relate to the above criminal activity should be shared with DCSA. More specifically, the types of records and information that fall under the legal definition of CHRI include (but are not necessarily limited to) the following:[36]

- copies of police reports
- notations of the date and place of an offense
- statement of the actual charge
- descriptions of the circumstances related to the event
- disposition of the crime
- outstanding warrants
- open arrests
- pending criminal charges
- nolle prosequi determinations
- not guilty determinations
- dismissals
- parole or probation records
- expungements
- sealed records.

While these lists primarily focus on records and information related to specific violations of law, DCSA requires further information to complete its background investigations—specifically, information on alleged or suspected criminal activity. This information is required to obtain a complete profile of an individual subject's trustworthiness, particularly when investigators interview subjects concerning these events in their past. Since DCSA conducts background investigations for federal positions of trust and to permit access to sensitive federal information, it must be aware of all potential areas of concern regarding an individual's suitability. By providing the most complete and comprehensive records available, criminal justice and law enforcement agencies play a critical role in ensuring the safety and security of the federal workforce.[37]

Chapter Five
How Do DCSA Staff Perform Their Duties?

DCSA requests for CHRI from law enforcement and criminal justice agencies are one step of the overall investigative and adjudicative process for determining a subject's suitability or fitness for federal employment and access to sensitive information. Figure 5 shows the different phases of this larger process, from initiation to investigation to adjudication.

The investigative process begins when federal agencies submit requests for investigations to DCSA for current or prospective employees or contractors (i.e., the subjects of the investigations). DCSA sends the agencies' requested subjects an electronic questionnaire, the SF-86 form, in which they supply personal and employment information to aid in the investigation. Based on this information, DCSA schedules and then initiates the investigation by conducting automated record checks. The record checks access various law enforcement and criminal justice databases, such as the FBI National Crime Information Center database. DCSA also automatically sends out inquiry forms (INV Form 44), the first step in the CHRI sharing process described below.

Next, DCSA agents complete fieldwork, as needed, to address any gaps in information determined by their initial inquiries and the information provided by the subject. The CHRI sharing process with law enforcement and criminal justice agencies occurs during this step, as highlighted in Figure 5. Once all information on a subject is collected, DCSA agents review the case before sending the Report of Investigation to agencies for adjudication. Agencies then determine whether the subject meets the requirements for federal employment and/or access to sensitive information. The agencies report their decision to DCSA. The subject is then enrolled in a continuous evaluation and vetting system, ensuring the continued suitability of employees throughout their time in federal service.[38]

During the investigation phase of the process, DCSA's investigators collect CHRI from SLTT agencies in two steps.

Step One. DCSA headquarters personnel send investigative (or inquiry) request forms (INV Form 44) to relevant law enforcement and criminal justice agencies. To identify which SLTT agencies to send the inquiry forms to, headquarters personnel use both database checks and a subject's provided history in their SF-86 form. The SF-86 compiles information on the subject's personal and employment history. With that information, DCSA then identifies the law enforcement and criminal justice agencies that may have the subject's CHRI on file.[39]

For instance, if a subject lived in Boston while attending college, DCSA would send requests for CHRI to the city's police department and the university's security department. DCSA mails the inquiry forms to the identified agencies, asking them to complete the form and send relevant documentation related to the subject's details. The current investigative request form includes sections to input offenses, law enforcement agency or court names, claimed residence at the time of offense(s), and details from the subject's criminal history record, including outstanding warrants, disposition dates, and locations of disposition. The form also contains an open-ended section for any other details that may be pertinent to the subject's eligibility for federal employment. If the identified agency sends the completed form and supporting CHRI documents back to DCSA, the process ends there.[40] If DCSA does not receive a sufficiently complete response from the agency (i.e., a completed INV Form 44 with the appropriate CHRI attached), the second step is initiated.

Step Two. If DCSA does not receive a completed investigative request form and accompanying documentation, then it initiates an investigator check. These checks require individual DCSA investigators, either federal or contractor personnel, to dispatch to the criminal justice or law enforcement agencies to directly collect the CHRI. Most of these checks consist of the investigator visiting the agency in person and following the agency's protocols for requesting CHRI. Depending on the agency's preferred CHRI request methods, however, investigators may also make the requests through the mail, fax, phone, email, or internet portal.[41] For instance, some city police departments grant DCSA access to their databases that house CHRI for their designated areas. This access allows DCSA to retrieve CHRI on subjects without having to go through the police department each time.[42]

| 15 |

Figure 5. DCSA Vetting and Background Investigation Steps and Processes

INITIATION
Initiating agency determines investigation requirement

- 100+ agencies including DoD, DHS, VA, DOE, DOJ, HHS
- Applicant submits electronic questionnaire

INVESTIGATION
DCSA conducts background investigation

- Investigation scheduled
- Automated record checks are conducted
- Fieldwork is conducted
- Case reviewed

Law enforcement–DCSA information-sharing

ADJUDICATION
Initiating agency makes an adjudicative determination

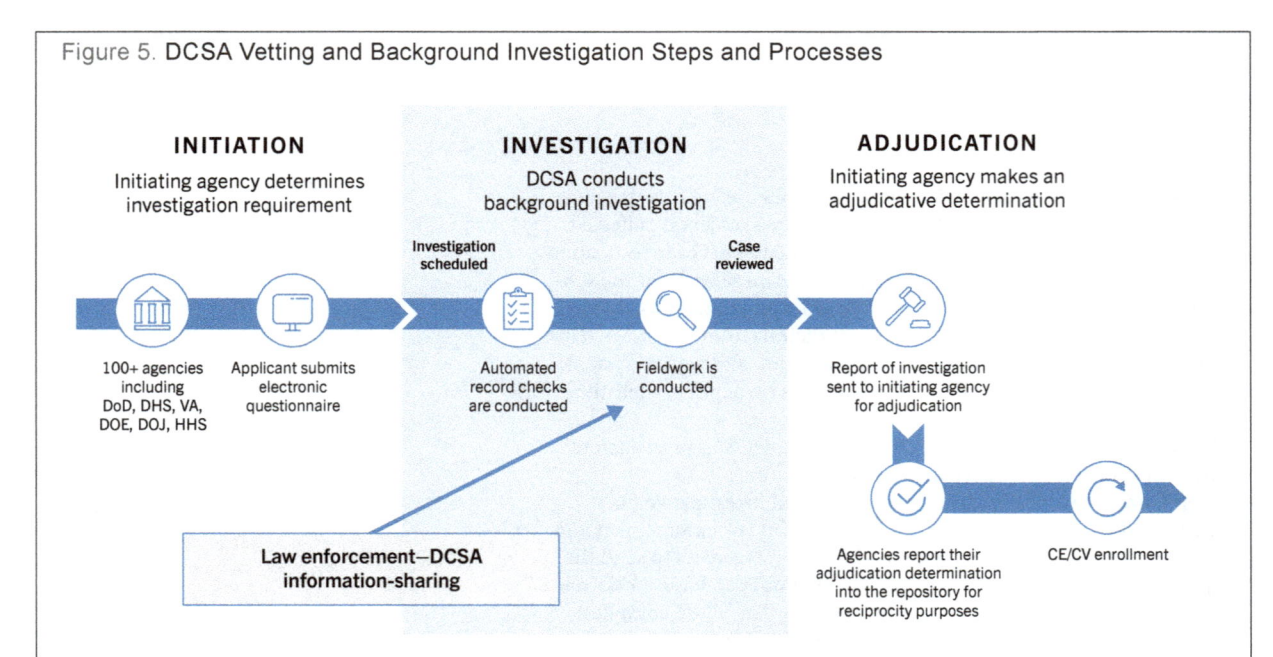

- Report of investigation sent to initiating agency for adjudication
- Agencies report their adjudication determination into the repository for reciprocity purposes
- CE/CV enrollment

SOURCE: DCSA, 2020b.
NOTE: CE/CV = Continuous Evaluation/Continuous Vetting; DHS = Department of Homeland Security; DOE = Department of Energy; DOJ = Department of Justice; HHS = Department of Health and Human Services.

When DCSA investigators conduct the checks in person, they will approach agency representatives to state their request. They may present their business cards and badges to prove that they represent DCSA. DCSA federal personnel carry gold badges, while contract investigators carry silver badges. If the investigator makes the request through written means (mail, email, fax), they will supply their DCSA investigator identification number. Law enforcement agencies can use this number to confirm the identity of the investigator and ensure that they work for DCSA and should be granted access to the information. DCSA provides a toll-free number that agency representatives can call to confirm investigator status. Many times, DCSA investigators work in the same region over an extended period so that agency representatives can personally identify DCSA investigators without needing to confirm their identity.[43]

In addition to their credentials, investigators will have a signed consent form from the subject being investigated. This form states that the subject knows that the investigation is being conducted, and they agree to DCSA accessing their information. The investigator can provide this consent form to the law enforcement or criminal justice agency, as needed or upon request.[44] Once DCSA investigators receive the required CHRI for the subject, the CHRI sharing process is complete. All information concerning the subject (applicant for a federal position) is compiled for the purposes of continuing the vetting process: interviews, adjudications, and decisions.

Chapter Six
How Can CHRI Sharing with DCSA Be Made Easier?

Background investigations, personnel vetting, and the CHRI sharing operations are resource-intensive and time-consuming operations for both the federal government and SLTT law enforcement agency partners. DCSA's objective is to assist its SLTT law enforcement agency partners with CHRI sharing to the greatest extent possible. To that end, DCSA offers four mechanisms through which CHRI sharing with DCSA can be made easier, more efficient, and more effective.

1. DCSA has created a suite of training materials and tools to facilitate knowledge transfer and development. DCSA headquarters and field personnel distribute these materials and tools nationwide and offer person-to-person training to SLTT law enforcement agency jurisdictions that request such training.
2. DCSA field staff are ready, willing, and able (i.e., they maintain sufficient security clearances) to apply for and accept access to local SLTT CHRI databases. By providing direct access, SLTT jurisdictions can save considerable resources and time by shifting the burden of CHRI collection and sharing directly to DCSA personnel.
3. DCSA provides sample language that SLTT law enforcement agency jurisdictions may incorporate into their own regulations, policy memorandum, and training programs to inform staff of

| 17 |

DCSA's investigative and CHRI authorities. Incorporating such language reduces SLTT staff confusion or concern over DCSA's authorities and procedures, which facilitates the building of rapport and CHRI sharing activities.
4. DCSA leaders, managers, and investigators are prepared to brief state attorneys general offices and county and local attorneys on DCSA, its organization, and its authorities should SLTT law enforcement agencies require written or verbal confirmation that CHRI sharing with DCSA is permissible under all state and local laws, regulations, and policies.

Providing SLTTs with DCSA Outreach Education and Training Materials and Tools

To better assist SLTT criminal justice and law enforcement partners, DCSA developed a suite of outreach tools and materials designed to both educate and train SLTT leaders, managers, and staff at all levels on how to more effectively and efficiently share CHRI. These tools and materials are designed to (1) facilitate different modes of education and training and (2) provide easy and clear notifications and instructions to SLTT partner staff so that they may quickly understand DCSA as an organization, its mission and authorities, its staff, its CHRI needs, and the best methods for sharing CHRI. These tools and materials include the following:

- this guidebook
- training presentation
- fact sheet
- frequently asked questions
- one-pagers
- brochures
- posters
- email blast.

You may obtain any of the above materials from your local DCSA investigators or field staff. Additionally, you may request a training session from your local DCSA field office or from DCSA's LELO. DCSA personnel will be happy to provide in-person training and/or additional explanation and discussion with respect to any of the above materials.

Providing DCSA Staff with Access Privileges to SLTT Criminal and Court Databases

Departments and agencies that do not have sufficient staff to respond to DCSA CHRI requests in a timely manner are authorized under federal law to provide DCSA personnel with direct access to their criminal justice and court record databases. With respect to DCSA's authority for being granted such access, 5 U.S.C. 9101 states the following:

- A State central criminal history record depository shall allow a covered agency to conduct both biometric and biographic searches of criminal history record information.[45]
- Automated information delivery systems shall be used to provide criminal history record information to a covered agency under subsection (b) whenever available.[46]
- Fees, if any, charged for automated access through such systems may not exceed the reasonable cost of providing such access.[47]
- The criminal justice agency providing the criminal history record information through such systems may not limit disclosure on the basis that the repository is accessed from outside the State.[48]
- Information provided through such systems shall be the full and complete criminal history record.[49]
- Criminal justice agencies shall accept and respond to requests for criminal history record information through such systems with printed or photocopied records when requested.[50]
- If a criminal justice agency is able to provide the same information through more than 1 system described in paragraph (1), a covered agency may request information under subsection (b) from the criminal justice agency, and require the criminal justice agency to provide the information, using the system that is most cost-effective for the Federal Government.[51]

In practice, some SLTT criminal justice and law enforcement departments, agencies, and courts frequently provide DCSA staff (investigators or investigative assistants) with access to their local CHRI databases.[52] In addition to statutory authorization, DCSA personnel have sufficient background investigations and U.S. Government clearances to become users of local criminal justice, law enforcement, and court databases. If your database managers require that certain trainings be completed by individuals prior to gaining access, or if other procedures need to be followed, DCSA staff will ensure appropriate compliance with these conditions.

Providing SLTTs with Language to Incorporate in Their Records Manuals or Policy Guidance, Notifications, Instructions, and Training Programs

In some instances, SLTT criminal justice and law enforcement departments and agencies have incorporated language into their own authorities documents to notify, instruct, and train their staff on how to share CHRI with DCSA.[53] These jurisdictions have reported that providing this information to their personnel has allowed them to ensure compliance with federal law while also aiding their staff in developing procedures and processes to more effectively and efficiently share CHRI with DCSA investigators. Additionally, incorporating such language has also helped SLTT and DCSA staff to forge stronger relationships and develop CHRI sharing networks across SLTT jurisdictions. For example, sample language for incorporation into a CHRI sharing policy memorandum is as follows:

- When listing out criminal justice agencies for whom your office provides CHRI on a regular basis, be sure to include DCSA. Although DCSA is not a law enforcement agency, its background investigations are an authorized law enforcement activity. A sample list of federal agencies (including DCSA, highlighted below) might be
    1. U.S. Department of Justice, Bureau of Alcohol, Tobacco, Firearms and Explosives
    2. U.S. Customs and Border Protection
    3. U.S. Department of State, Diplomatic Security Service
    4. U.S. Drug Enforcement Administration
    5. Federal Bureau of Investigation
    6. Internal Revenue Service
    7. Office of Special Investigations
    8. U.S. Postal Inspection Service
    9. U.S. Secret Service
    10. U.S. District Attorney
    11. U.S. Marshals Service
    12. U.S. Parole Commission
    13. U.S. Probation Office
    14. Central Intelligence Agency
    15. U.S. Department of Justice
    16. U.S. Department of Homeland Security
    17. U.S. Department of Veterans Affairs Federal Police
    18. U.S. Department of Labor
    19. Military branches with criminal investigative and enforcement powers
    20. Defense Counterintelligence and Security Agency.[54]

- Provide directions (sample language follows) to records and other staff to treat DCSA requests in the same manner as a request from a criminal justice agency:

Criminal Justice Agency Requests (and the Defense Counterintelligence and Security Agency [DCSA])

Police records and criminal history records information (CHRI) requests by criminal justice agencies must be directed to the [*insert office or records unit*] if the request is for employment background purposes and must include an authorization for release of information signed by the subject/applicant. Only [*insert your department/agency name*] records and CHRI will be disseminated. Personal information of individuals other than the subject/applicant shall be redacted from the report(s) to include date of birth, address, phone, driver's license, and place of employment. The records may be faxed to the agency's official fax number, picked up from the [insert office or records unit] by the requesting individual, mailed by U.S. Postal Service to the agency's official address, or sent to the individual requesting the records using [insert preferred secure file transfer or encrypted email system] and to the individual's official work email address.

Criminal justice agencies and the Defense Counterintelligence and Security Agency (DCSA) may request police records for the purpose of criminal justice or national security activities directly from the [insert office or records unit] or the [insert any other applicable office or unit such as a crimes analysis unit, intelligence unit, etc.]. These reports shall not be redacted. These requests [insert "do/do not need to be entered into the records request database or the dissemination log" if applicable]. The records may be faxed to the agency's official fax number, picked up from the [insert office or records unit] by the requesting individual, mailed by U.S. Postal Service to the agency's official address, or sent to the individual requesting the records using [insert preferred secure file transfer or encrypted email system] and to the individual's official work email address.[55]

| 21 |

Providing SLTTs with Confirmation from State/County/Local Attorney or State Attorney General's Office of DCSA's Authority to Request CHRI

As described in Chapter Two, DCSA has broad legal authority to collect CHRI from SLTT criminal justice and law enforcement departments or agencies (see Appendix A). SLTT departments and agencies may request an advisor or an opinion from their state, county, or local attorney or state attorney general's office to confirm that DCSA's federal authorities supersede all SLTT laws regarding CHRI disclosures.

Local field DCSA Special Agents-in-Charge and investigators, as well as officials from the DCSA LELO, can provide your state, county, or local attorney or state attorney general's office with the necessary legal information to make this determination. These DCSA officials are also available to speak and/or meet with your local legal authorities and advisors to facilitate the issuance of these confirmations of DCSA's background investigation and CHRI request authorities.

Appendix A. DCSA Statutory and Executive Order Authorities

DCSA is statutorily empowered to collect CHRI. It derives the authority to collect CHRI from several sources, including law and multiple executive orders. These laws are summarized as follows:

U.S. Code, Title 5, Section 9101: Access to Criminal History Records for National Security and Other Purposes

This statute grants DCSA the authority to request and receive CHRI from criminal justice agencies for the purpose of conducting background investigations. *Criminal justice agency* is defined as any federal, state, or local agency that performs the administration of criminal justice and federal, state, or local courts. Title 5 discusses "covered agencies," specific to this need, as organizations that are authorized to collect CHRI, including DoD and contracted employees.

Title 5 of the U.S. Code also defines criminal history record information as follows:

> information collected by criminal justice agencies on individuals consisting of identifiable descriptions and notations of arrests, indictments, informations, or other formal criminal charges, and any disposition arising therefrom, sentencing, correction supervision, and release. The term does not include identification information such as fingerprint records to the extent that such information does not indicate involvement of the individual in the criminal justice system. The term includes those records of a State or locality sealed pursuant to law if such records are accessible by State and local criminal justice agencies for the purpose of conducting background checks.

Some law enforcement agencies may, understandably, question whether they are allowed to share the detailed information required by DCSA for its investigations. Rest assured, 5 U.S.C. 9101 provides that law enforcement agencies have no liability for legally releasing CHRI to DCSA within guidelines of the law.

List of authorities, for reference: 5 U.S.C. 9101; the Civil Service Rules of Executive Order 10577, as amended;[56] 5 U.S.C. 3301 and 7301;[57] 5 C.F.R. Part 731; Executive Order 13467, as amended; 50 U.S.C. 3341(c); Executive Order 12968, as amended;[58] Executive Order 13869.

- Executive Order 13467: Reforming Processes Related to Suitability for Government Employment, Fitness for Contractor Employees, and Eligibility for Access to Classified National Security Information (June 30, 2008)
    - This executive order was extensively amended by Executive Order 13869, 2019.
    - This executive order designates DCSA as "the primary entity for conducting effective, efficient, and secure background investigations for the federal government."[59]
    - This executive order directed the transfer of the investigative functions, resources, and personnel of the OPM's NBIB to DCSA.

Appendix B. Data Collection Forms

This appendix contains an example of the current inquiry or bubble sheet DCSA uses to collect information. Note that it is still branded as an OPM form. This form is likely to evolve under DCSA; once that is complete, please update this page and replace it with the new form.

INV FORM 44 (Rev. 6/14)
U.S. OFFICE OF PERSONNEL MANAGEMENT (5 CFR 736)

INVESTIGATIVE REQUEST FOR LAW ENFORCEMENT DATA
U.S. GOVERNMENT USE ONLY

LAW ITEM (LAWE)

FROM:
UNITED STATES OFFICE OF PERSONNEL MANAGEMENT
FEDERAL INVESTIGATIONS PROCESSING CENTER
PO BOX 618
BOYERS, PA 16018-0618

TO:

INSTRUCTIONS: We are conducting a background investigation on the person identified below to determine this person's eligibility for federal employment or access to classified information. To help make this determination, we ask that you complete all items on the back of this form and return the form in the enclosed envelope.

PRIVACY ACT INFORMATION: This investigative inquiry is in full compliance with the Privacy Act of 1974 and other laws protecting the civil rights of the person we are investigating. The information you provide, including your identity, will be disclosed to the person being investigated and other federal agencies, at this person's request.

CERTIFICATION: The person we are investigating has given written consent for this investigative inquiry. We keep that consent on file. If a copy is required in order to complete this form, please indicate this requirement in writing on the reverse.

The U.S. Office of Personnel Management's Federal Investigations Program is an authorized law enforcement activity required by Statute, Presidential Executive Order and Federal Regulations to make this investigative inquiry.

☐ Request covered by the Security Clearance Information Act (P.L. 99-169)
☐ Request not covered by the Security Clearance Information Act

Completion of this form as soon as possible will help this person and the agency perform their duties in a more timely and efficient manner.

CASE NUMBER: CASE TYPE: ITEM NUMBER:

FULL NAME (LAST, FIRST, MIDDLE)

OTHER NAMES USED

DATE OF BIRTH   SOCIAL SECURITY NUMBER   POSITION REQUIRING INVESTIGATION

PLACE OF BIRTH

CURRENT RESIDENCE

THIS PERSON CLAIMS THE FOLLOWING CRIMINAL HISTORY RECORD AT YOUR LOCATION

DATE (MO/YR)	DATE (MO/YR)
OFFENSE:	OFFENSE:
ACTION:	ACTION:

LAW ENFORCEMENT AUTHORITY OR COURT

CLAIMED RESIDENCE AT TIME OF OFFENSE

U.S. GOVERNMENT PRINTING OFFICE 2019-404-320/40350   221435-4   FORM APPROVED: OMB:3206-0165

| 25 |

MARKING INSTRUCTIONS

CORRECT MARK: ●

- USE A NO. 2 PENCIL OR BLUE OR BLACK INK PEN ONLY.
- DO NOT USE PENS WITH INK THAT SOAKS THROUGH THE PAPER.
- DO NOT MAKE ANY STRAY MARKS ON THIS SHEET.

INCORRECT MARKS: ✗ ✓ · —

PLEASE COMPLETE THE ITEMS SHOWN BELOW

1 MARK THE FOLLOWING AS APPLICABLE:

a. WE HAVE NO RECORD ON THIS PERSON.   b. RECORD INFORMATION SHOWN BELOW.

2 PLEASE PROVIDE DETAILS CONCERNING CRIMINAL HISTORY RECORD AND/OR OUTSTANDING WARRANT(S).
IF OUTSTANDING WARRANT(S) EXIST, LIST THE NATURE OF THE ORIGINAL CHARGE.
PLEASE SHOW THE EXACT NATURE OF THE CHARGE - <u>DO NOT USE CODES OR ABBREVIATIONS.</u>

DATE	OFFENSE	DISPOSITION AND DATE	LOCATION OF DISPOSITION (COURT & CITY)

3 IF ADDITIONAL INFORMATION IS PROVIDED BELOW, YOU MUST FILL IN THIS MARK.

REMARKS, ADDITIONAL INFORMATION THAT MAY HAVE A BEARING ON THIS PERSON'S ELIGIBILITY FOR FEDERAL EMPLOYMENT, ACCESS TO CLASSIFIED INFORMATION OR ASSIGNMENT TO SENSITIVE NATIONAL SECURITY DUTIES.

PUBLIC BURDEN INFORMATION: We estimate the Public Burden for this collection of information is approximately 5 minutes per response. This includes time for reviewing the instructions, gathering the information requested, and completing and returning the form. You may send comments regarding our estimate or any other aspect of this form, including suggestions for reducing completion time, to the Office of Personnel Management, Forms Officer, Paperwork Reduction Act (3206-0165), Washington, DC 20415-7900. The OMB Number 3206-0165 is currently valid. OPM may not collect this information, and you are not required to respond, unless this number is displayed. Do not send your completed form to this address.

PRINT NAME:

SIGNATURE: | **DATE**

YOUR TITLE/ORGANIZATION: | **DAYTIME TELEPHONE NUMBER (INCLUDE AREA CODE)** ( )

FOR OPM USE ONLY

RESULTS

- AC ACCEPTABLE
- AA ACCEPTABLE/ATTACHED
- PA CONFIDENTIAL/ACCEPTABLE
- NI NO PERTINENT INFORMATION
- NR NO RECORD
- NL NOT LOCATED
- UC UNABLE TO CONTACT
- RF REFERRED
- RR RECORD

- IS ISSUES
- PI CONFIDENTIAL/ISSUES
- RI RECORD INCONCLUSIVE
- FR FEE REQUIRED
- RL RELEASE REQUIRED
- SK SUBJECT UNKNOWN
- NZ NOT AVAILABLE
- DN DISCREPANT

ISSUES/CHARACTERIZATION

1 ○ A B C D E N   9 ○ A B C D E N
2 ○ A B C D E N   10 ○ A B C D E N
3 ○ A B C D E N   11 ○ A B C D E N
4 ○ A B C D E N   12 ○ A B C D E N
5 ○ A B C D E N   13 ○ A B C D E N
6 ○ A B C D E N   14 ○ A B C D E N
7 ○ A B C D E N
8 ○ A B C D E N

| 26 |

Appendix C. U.S. Department of Justice Letter to State and Local Law Enforcement Agencies and Courts

The U.S. Department of Justice has issued guidance to SLTT criminal justice and law enforcement agencies and courts to facilitate their compliance with the requirements for CHRI sharing under federal law. We provide a copy of this guidance in this appendix.

U.S. Department of Justice

Washington, D.C. 20530

Dear State and Local Law Enforcement Agencies and Courts:

Throughout the last decade, the Federal Government has experienced a number of insider threat events, including instances where classified national security information was released to the public. More alarmingly, individuals employed by the Federal Government have been wounded or killed while at federal facilities due to criminal acts by individuals previously vetted for employment with the Federal Government.

I am writing to you today to emphasize the importance of compliance with Title 5, United States Code Section 9101 – the federal law that requires the sharing of Criminal History Record Information (CHRI) with Federal Government Agencies for background investigation purposes.

After fatal incidents at places like Fort Hood, TX and the Washington Navy Yard, reviews commissioned by the President and Congress were conducted to identify vulnerabilities in policies and processes involving federal background investigations for civilians, military, and contractor personnel. A significant finding of these reviews showed there needs to be higher degree of compliance nationwide with 5 U.S.C. § 9101.

We're asking for your help. It is critical that federal, state, and local criminal justice agencies collaborate on CHRI sharing. We must reduce gaps in our current processes to ensure that we have the most complete and accurate background vetting program possible. This will guarantee that only the most trustworthy candidates are employed to protect our vital national security information, our people and this nation.

Some reasons cited for non-compliance were lack of funding and resources, the absence of up-to-date automated data systems, and policy barriers. If technical or budgetary barriers impede your ability to achieve full compliance with 5 U.S.C. § 9101, the National Criminal History Improvement Program and the Federal Emergency Management Agency Grant Program may be available to assist. Additional information providing background for this request and the statutory requirements discussed can be found in the Enclosure.

We appreciate all your efforts and your full cooperation in tackling this critical issue.

Sincerely,

Theophani Stamos
Law Enforcement Liaison, State and Local Law Enforcement Coordination Section

Enclosure

| 27 |

Statutory Requirements for Sharing Criminal History Record　　　　　　　　　ENCLOSURE
Information with Federal Background Investigators

BACKGROUND

In September 2013, following the Washington Navy Yard shootings, the President directed the Office of Management and Budget to conduct a comprehensive review of the Federal Government's employee suitability, contractor fitness, credentialing, and security clearance procedures.

At about the same time, Congress directed (in Section 907(f) of the National Defense Authorization Act for FY 2014) the Security, Suitability, and Credentialing (SSC) Performance Accountability Council (PAC)–the senior interagency group responsible to the President for SSC reform– to convene a Task Force on Records Access to examine the policies and procedures that determine the level of access to public records provided by State and local authorities in response to investigative requests by the Federal Government. Section 907(f)(4) directed the task force to provide recommendations to improve the degree of cooperation and records-sharing between State and local authorities and the Federal Government.

On February 28, 2014, the Suitability and Security Processes Review *Report to the President* was issued, and its recommendations were approved by the President on March 3, 2014.[1] One of the findings was that there needs to be a higher degree of compliance nationwide with the criminal history record information (CHRI) sharing requirements of 5 U.S.C. § 9101. Specifically, the Report noted that a relatively large percentage of State and local law enforcement entities had failed to fully comply with this law and recommended the PAC review relevant statutes to determine if changes were necessary. The Report also recommended Federal funding mechanisms be identified to encourage cooperation and compliance with existing statutes.

On May 9, 2014, the Records Access Task Force *Report to Congress* was issued, outlining its findings and recommendations, including the recommendation to amend 5 U.S.C. § 9101 and to establish a Federal Background Investigations Liaison Office.

ACTIONS TAKEN TO IMPROVE CHRI SHARING

Revisions to 5 U.S.C. § 9101, as recommended by the task force, were signed into law by the President on November 25, 2015. The revised law requires sharing CHRI with key Federal Government agencies for background investigations conducted for national security, public trust, employment and suitability/fitness purposes on behalf of the Executive branch. *(The revised requirements are provided on Page 2.)*

On October 1st, 2019, the Office of Personnel Management's National Background Investigations Bureau (NBIB) merged with the Department of Defense's Defense Security Services forming the Defense Counterintelligence and Security Agency (DCSA). The DCSA established the Federal Law Enforcement Liaison Office (LELO) to oversee education initiatives, resolve issues that may develop between Federal investigative service providers and State and local criminal justice agencies, and promote CHRI sharing.

IMPORTANCE OF SHARING CHRI

When State or local criminal justice agencies are uable to fully comply with 5 U.S.C. § 9101, it poses substantial challenges for Federal Government decision makers. Missing or incomplete CHRI in Federal background investigations could result in someone being approved for a public trust or sensitive position with the Federal Government, or gain access to classified national security information, in error, which poses an unacceptable risk to the national security and to the protection of people, property, and information.

---

[1] The Security and Suitability Processes Review *Report to the President*, dated February 2014, can be found at https://obamawhitehouse.archives.gov/sites/default/files/omb/reports/suitability-and-security-process-review-report.pdf

| 28 |

5 U.S.C. § 9101, CHRI SHARING REQUIREMENTS

5 U.S.C. § 9101, as amended, mandates that:

Upon request by a covered agency, criminal justice agencies shall make available all criminal history record information regarding individuals under investigation by that covered agency, in accordance with Federal Investigative Standards jointly promulgated by the Suitability Executive Agent and Security Executive Agent, for the purpose of-

(A) determining eligibility for-
 (i) access to classified information;
 (ii) assignment to or retention in sensitive national security duties or positions;
 (iii) acceptance or retention in the armed forces; or
 (iv) appointment, retention, or assignment to a position of public trust while either employed by the Government or performing a Government contract; or
(B) conducting a basic suitability or fitness assessment for Federal or contractor employees, using Federal Investigative Standards jointly promulgated by the Security Executive Agent and the Suitability Executive Agent in accordance with-
 (i) Executive Order 13467 (73 Federal Register 38103), or any successor thereto; and
 (ii) the Office of Management and Budget memorandum "Assignment of Functions Relating to Coverage of Contractor Employee Fitness in the Federal Investigative Standards", dated December 6, 2012;
(C) credentialing under the Homeland Security Presidential Directive 12 (dated August 27, 2004); and
(D) Federal Aviation Administration checks required under-
 (i) the Federal Aviation Administration Drug Enforcement Assistance Act of 1988 (subtitle E of title VII of Public Law 100-690; 102 Stat. 4424) and the amendments made by that Act; or
 (ii) section 44710 of title 49.

FEDERAL PROGRAMS THAT CAN HELP

The National Criminal History Improvement Program (NCHIP) provides financial assistance to improve the quality, timeliness, and immediate accessibility of criminal history records and related information to enhance information sharing. This program is managed by the Department of Justice, Office of Justice Programs, Bureau of Justice Statistics (BJS). The NCHIP accepts applications for financial assistance on an annual basis; information about this program is available at https://www.bjs.gov/content/pub/pdf/nchip20_sol.pdf. Agencies with open NCHIP awards can reach out directly to BJS to discuss how current awarded funds may be used to comply with this law.

The Department of Homeland Security has also identified the Federal Emergency Management Agency Grant Program as another source of financial assistance to help your agencies automate their CHRI to share with the Federal Government. Information regarding this grant program may be found at https://www.fema.gov/non-disaster-grants-management-system.

Appendix D. DCSA Organization Nationwide

This appendix provides additional information regarding the personnel size and makeup and the location of DCSA's Field Operations division and relevant headquarters' offices (i.e., FIRE, Quality Assurance, and Customer and Stakeholder Engagement).

Figure D.1. BI Field and Staffing Structure

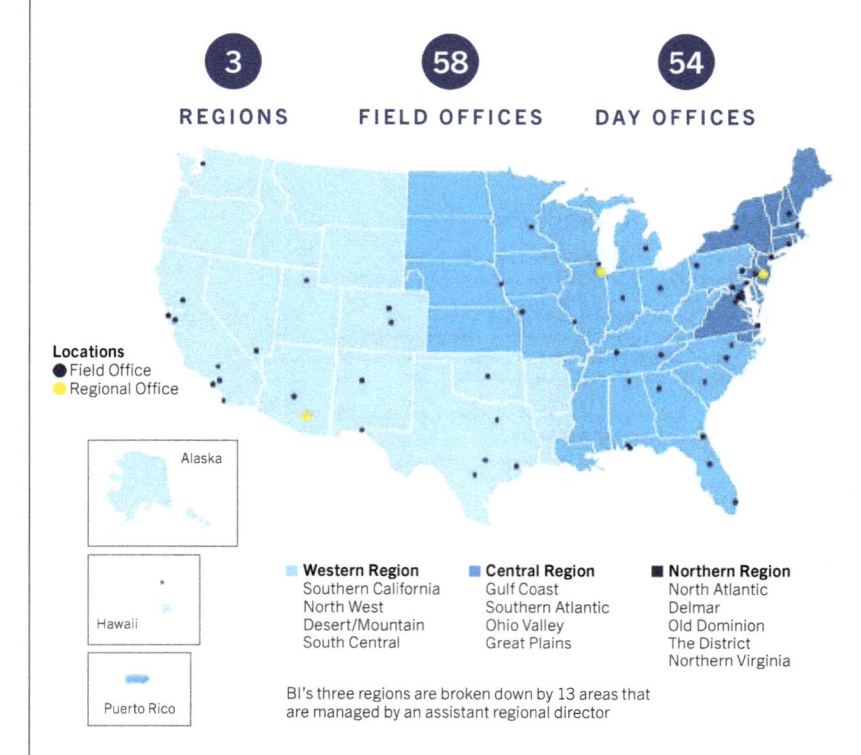

3 REGIONS   **58** FIELD OFFICES   **54** DAY OFFICES

Locations
- Field Office
- Regional Office

Western Region
Southern California
North West
Desert/Mountain
South Central

Central Region
Gulf Coast
Southern Atlantic
Ohio Valley
Great Plains

Northern Region
North Atlantic
Delmar
Old Dominion
The District
Northern Virginia

BI's three regions are broken down by 13 areas that are managed by an assistant regional director

Staffing at a Glance

FIELD OPERATIONS
- 3 regional directors
- 13 assistant regional directors
- 96 Supervisory Agents-in-Charge
- 1,587 federal investigators
- 100 investigative assistants
- 5,075 field contract staff

FIRE
- 130 federal employees
- 1,010 contract support staff

QUALITY
- 470 federal employees
- 15 contract support staff

CUSTOMER & STAKEHOLDER ENGAGEMENT
- 41 federal employees

MISSION SUPPORT
- 27 federal employees
- 9 contract support staff

SOURCE: DCSA, 2020b, updated 2021 (v6).

| 30 |

Appendix E. DCSA Contact Information

- For questions related to an agent or investigator's identity, position, and authority, contact the DCSA Safety and Security Team at (888) 795-5673, Monday through Friday, 7 a.m.–4 p.m. ET.
- For questions about DCSA and its partnership with law enforcement agencies, contact the DCSA Law Enforcement Liaison Office at (202) 606-1606 or DCSA.Law-Enforcement-Liaison@mail.mil.
- For assistance with completing investigative request forms, contact DCSA Records Outreach at (724) 794-5612.

Abbreviations

ADJ	adjudications
BI	background investigations
CHRI	criminal history record information
CI	counterintelligence
CSC	Civil Service Commission
CTP	critical technology protection
DCSA	Defense Counterintelligence and Security Agency
DIS	Defense Investigative Service
DITMAC	DoD Insider Threat Management and Analysis Center
DoD	U.S. Department of Defense
FBI	Federal Bureau of Investigation
FIRE	Federal Investigative Records Enterprise
LELO	Law Enforcement Liaison Office
NBIB	National Background Investigations Bureau
NBIS	National Background Investigative Service
OPM	Office of Personnel Management
SLTT	state, local, tribal, and territorial
VRO	vetting risk operations

Endnotes

[1] "Defense Security Service," *DCSAACCESS*, Vol. 8, No. 4, 2019.

[2] Executive Order 13869, Transferring Responsibility for Background Investigations to the Department of Defense, Washington, D.C., April 24, 2019.

[3] "History of the Agency," *DCSAACCESS*, Vol. 8, No. 4, 2019; Executive Order 13869, 2019.

[4] David Hicks, "Criminal Justice Agencies and Department of Defense/DCSA First Line of Defense Against Insider Threats," newsletter, July 2020; DCSA, "About Us," webpage, undated-a.

[5] DCSA, undated-a.

[6] DCSA, "Mission, Vision, and Values," webpage, undated-e.

[7] DCSA, "Background Investigations," webpage, undated-b.

[8] DCSA, "Criminal Justice and the U.S. Department of Defense: Safeguarding Integrity in Federal Background Investigations," brochure, undated-c.

[9] DCSA, undated-c; Hicks, 2020.

[10] William K. Lietzau, "DCSA Command/Mission Briefing," May 3, 2021.

[11] DCSA, undated-b.

[12] DCSA, "BI-Organizational Chart," updated July 22, 2020a.

[13] DCSA, "DCSA Background Investigations Overview," briefing slides, September 22, 2020b.

[14] DCSA, 2020b; interviews with 13 Special Agents-in-Charge conducted during June and July 2021.

[15] Interviews with DCSA officials, January 19, 2021, and March 23, 2021.

[16] DCSA, undated-c.

[17] David Hicks, "Criminal Justice Agencies and Department of Defense/DCSA National Background Investigations First Line of Defense Against Insider Threats," presentation to field staff, undated-b; interview with DCSA official, February 1, 2021.

[18] DCSA, 2020b.

[19] U.S. Code, Title 5, Section 9101, Access to criminal history records for national security and other purposes, January 23, 2000, (a)(6)(J).

[20] DCSA, "Verification of Email Requests: Verify the Authenticity of an Email Request for an Interview or Information," webpage, undated-f.

[21] Cybersecurity and Infrastructure Security Agency, "Defining Insider Threats," webpage, undated; and DCSA, "Insider Threat," webpage, undated-d.

[22] DCSA, undated-c.

[23] U.S. Department of Justice, "U.S. Attorney's Office Closes Investigation Involving Fatal Shooting of Aaron Alexis: No Charges to Be Filed Against Officers Who Responded to Mass Murders at Washington Navy Yard," press release, Washington, D.C., August 27, 2014.

[24] Hicks, undated-b; Committee on Oversight and Government Reform, *Slipping Through the Cracks: How the D.C. Navy Yard Shooting Exposes Flaws in the Federal Security Clearance Process*, U.S. House of Representatives, Washington, D.C., February 11, 2014, pp. 4–12.

[25] See *U.S. v. California*, case number 06-cv-2649, Not Reported in F.Supp.2d, 2007 WL 3341670 United States District Court, E.D. California, November 8, 2007. In this litigation between the State of California and the U.S. Government (and OPM, which was the office conducting federal background investigations at the time) the Federal District Court held that 5 U.S.C. 9101 preempts state and local laws with regard to the disclosure of CHRI. Therefore, if a state or local law restricts disclosure of CHRI, that restriction cannot be applied to the U.S. government (and/or DCSA or other properly designated federal agency) for the purposes of its background investigations.

[26] See 5 U.S.C. 9101(b)(1) and (e)(1) through (e)(6).

[27] See 5 U.S.C. 9101(b)(4).

[28] See 5 U.S.C. 9101(a)(2).

[29] See 5 U.S.C. 9101(b)(1)(A) through (D); Homeland Security Presidential Directive 12, *Policy for a Common Identification Standard for Federal Employees and Contractors*, Washington, D.C., August 27, 2004.

[30] U.S. Code, Title 50, Section 3341, Security clearances.

[31] U.S. Code, Title 10, Section 1564, Security clearance investigations.

[32] Executive Order 13467, Reforming Processes Related to Suitability for Government Employment, Fitness for Contractor Employees, and Eligibility for Access to Classified National Security Information, Washington, D.C., June 30, 2008.

[33] Executive Order 13869, 2019.

[34] Code of Federal Regulations, Title 5, Part 731, Suitability.

[35] See, generally, Federal Investigative Services Division, *Investigator's Handbook,* U.S. Office of Personnel Management, Washington, D.C., May 25, 2007, pp. 2-38, 3-147, 4-214, 5-249 to 5-250, 7-321, 8-340, 8-513, and 8-521.

[36] Federal Investigative Services Division, 2007.

[37] David Hicks, "Criminal Justice Agencies and Department of Defense/DCSA National Background Investigations First Line of Defense Against Insider Threats," presentation to criminal justice agencies, undated-a; DCSA, undated-c; and Committee on Oversight and Government Reform, 2014, pp. 40–43. See also Appendix C, open letter to all state and local law enforcement agencies and courts, U.S. Department of Justice, enclosure.

[38] DCSA, 202b; DCSA, undated-c.

[39] Interviews with DCSA officials, February 11, 2021, and April 8, 2021.

[40] Interviews with DCSA officials, February 11, 2021, April 8, 2021, May 4, 2021, and May 18, 2021; and INV Form 44, Investigative Request for Law Enforcement Data, U.S. Office of Personnel Management, undated.

| 33 |

[41] Interviews with DCSA officials, February 11, 2021, April 14, 2021, May 18, 2021, and July 19, 2021, and interview with SLTT law enforcement officials, August 12, 2021.

[42] Interviews with DCSA officials, April 14, 2021, April 19, 2021, July 9, 2021, and July 12, 2021.

[43] Hicks, undated-a; interviews with DCSA officials, February 11, 2021, April 14, 2021, June 30, 2021, and July 6, 2021; interview with SLTT law enforcement officials, August 13, 2021.

[44] Hicks, undated-b; interviews with DCSA officials, February 11, 2021, May 4, 2021, and May 18, 2021.

[45] See 5 U.S.C. 9101(b)(2)(A).

[46] See 5 U.S.C. 9101(e)(1).

[47] See 5 U.S.C. 9101(e)(2).

[48] See 5 U.S.C. 9101(e)(3).

[49] See 5 U.S.C. 9101(e)(4).

[50] See 5 U.S.C. 9101(e)(5).

[51] See 5 U.S.C. 9101(e)(6).

[52] Interviews with DCSA officials, February 1, 2021, April 14, 2021, and April 19, 2021.

[53] Interviews with SLTT law enforcement officials, August 13, 2021.

[54] Adapted from data collected from SLTT interviews.

[55] Adapted from data collected from SLTT interviews.

[56] Executive Order 10577, Amending the Civil Service Rules and Authorizing a New Appointment System for the Competitive Service, Washington, D.C., as amended on multiple dates.

[57] U.S. Code, Title 5, Section 3301, Civil service; generally; and U.S. Code, Title 5, Section 7301, Presidential regulations.

[58] Executive Order 12968, Access to Classified Information, Washington, D.C., August 2, 1995.

[59] Executive Order 13467, 2008.

Credits

Design: Rick Penn-Kraus
Cover: Police: kali9/Getty Images; pen: _human/Getty Images/iStockphoto
Pg. iv: RyanJLane/Getty Images
Pg. 3: Kindel Media/Pexels
Pg. 6: LightFieldStudios/Getty Images/iStockphoto
Pg. 7: Михаил Руденко/Getty Images/iStockphoto
Pg. 9: fstop123/Getty Images/iStockphoto
Pg. 10: kali9/Getty Images/iStockphoto
Pg. 12: Doug Menuez/Getty Images
Pg. 14: ftwitty/Getty Images
Pg. 17: KatarzynaBialasiewicz/Getty Images/iStockphoto
Pg. 21: RichLegg/Getty Images/iStockphoto
Pg. 22: kali9/Getty Images

References

Code of Federal Regulations, Title 5, Part 731, Suitability.

Committee on Oversight and Government Reform, *Slipping Through the Cracks: How the D.C. Navy Yard Shooting Exposes Flaws in the Federal Security Clearance Process*, U.S. House of Representatives, Washington, D.C., February 11, 2014.

Cybersecurity and Infrastructure Security Agency, "Defining Insider Threats," webpage, undated. As of September 27, 2021:
https://www.cisa.gov/defining-insider-threats

DCSA—*See* Defense Counterintelligence and Security Agency.

Defense Counterintelligence and Security Agency, "About Us," webpage, undated-a. As of September 26, 2021:
https://www.dcsa.mil/about/

———, "Background Investigations," webpage, undated-b. As of September 26, 2021:
https://www.dcsa.mil/mc/pv/investigations/

———, "Criminal Justice and the U.S. Department of Defense: Safeguarding Integrity in Federal Background Investigations," brochure, undated-c.

———, "Insider Threat," webpage, undated-d. As of September 26, 2021:
https://www.dcsa.mil/mc/pv/insider_threat

———, "Mission, Vision, and Values," webpage, undated-e. As of September 26, 2021:
https://www.dcsa.mil/about/vision/

———, "Verification of Email Requests: Verify the Authenticity of an Email Request for an Interview or Information," webpage, undated-f. As of September 26, 2021:
https://www.dcsa.mil/mc/pv/mbi/vi/

———, "BI-Organizational Chart," updated July 22, 2020a.

———, "DCSA Background Investigations Overview," briefing slides, September 22, 2020b.

"Defense Security Service," *DCSA ACCESS*, Vol. 8, No. 4, 2019, pp. 14–15.

Executive Order 10577, Amending the Civil Service Rules and Authorizing a New Appointment System for the Competitive Service, Washington, D.C., as amended on multiple dates.

Executive Order 12968, Access to Classified Information, Washington, D.C., August 2, 1995.

Executive Order 13467, Reforming Processes Related to Suitability for Government Employment, Fitness for Contractor Employees, and Eligibility for Access to Classified National Security Information, Washington, D.C., June 30, 2008.

Executive Order 13869, Transferring Responsibility for Background Investigations to the Department of Defense, Washington, D.C., April 24, 2019.

Federal Investigative Services Division, *Investigator's Handbook*, U.S. Office of Personnel Management, Washington, D.C., May 25, 2007.

Hicks, David, "Criminal Justice Agencies and Department of Defense/DCSA National Background Investigations First Line of Defense Against Insider Threats," presentation to criminal justice agencies, undated-a.

———, "Criminal Justice Agencies and Department of Defense/DCSA National Background Investigations First Line of Defense Against Insider Threats," presentation to field staff, undated-b.

———, "Criminal Justice Agencies and Department of Defense/DCSA First Line of Defense Against Insider Threats," newsletter, July 2020.

"History of the Agency," *DCSAACCESS*, Vol. 8, No. 4, 2019, pp. 4–8.

Homeland Security Presidential Directive 12, *Policy for a Common Identification Standard for Federal Employees and Contractors*, Washington, D.C., August 27, 2004.

INV Form 44, Investigative Request for Law Enforcement Data, U.S. Office of Personnel Management, undated.

Lietzau, William K., "DCSA Command/Mission Briefing," May 3, 2021.

U.S. Code, Title 5, Section 3301, Civil service; generally.

U.S. Code, Title 5, Section 7301, Presidential regulations.

U.S. Code, Title 5, Section 9101, Access to criminal history records for national security and other purposes.

U.S. Code, Title 10, Section 1564, Security clearance investigations.

U.S. Code, Title 50, Section 3341, Security clearances.

U.S. Department of Justice, "U.S. Attorney's Office Closes Investigation Involving Fatal Shooting of Aaron Alexis: No Charges to Be Filed Against Officers Who Responded to Mass Murders at Washington Navy Yard," press release, Washington, D.C., August 27, 2014. As of September 26, 2021: https://www.justice.gov/usao-dc/pr/us-attorney-s-office-closes-investigation-involving-fatal-shooting-aaron-alexis-no

U.S. Versus California, U.S. District Court, E.D. California, November 8, 2007.

APPENDIX C

Frequently Asked Questions

The FAQ document provides key CHRI sharing information in a question-and-answer format drawn from the most frequently reported issues and questions that SLTT LEA personnel have regarding DCSA (and that have been reported by DCSA and/or SLTT LEA personnel):

- its organization, mission, and authorities
- the national security importance of CHRI sharing
- the processes and procedures employed by DCSA to conduct background investigations and CHRI collections
- common CHRI sharing impediments and solutions.

The FAQ is designed to assist DCSA field personnel during their interactions with SLTT LEA personnel as specific questions arise—questions that may vary from jurisdiction to jurisdiction according to the knowledge level, expertise, and particular areas of concern or interest.

Criminal Justice and the U.S. Department of Defense
Frequently Asked Questions

About the Defense Counterintelligence and Security Agency

Question: What is the Defense Counterintelligence and Security Agency (DCSA)?

Answer: DCSA is an agency within the U.S. Department of Defense (DoD). DCSA is the security agency in the federal government dedicated to protecting America's trusted workforce and trusted workspaces, whether physical or virtual. DCSA and its mission are critical components of the nation's security.

Question: What does DCSA do?

Answer: DCSA supports and secures the trustworthiness of the U.S. government's workforce through vetting, industry engagement, counterintelligence support, and education. As part of the vetting mission, DCSA conducts security, suitability, and fitness background investigations for access to classified information and nonsensitive positions for more than 2 million federal employees, federal contractors, and U.S. military personnel each year. DCSA investigators and DCSA's contract investigators collect criminal history record information (CHRI) as part of these investigations and vetting processes.

Question: Was there another agency that historically conducted personnel vetting?

Answer: Yes. Personnel vetting was previously conducted by the National Background Investigation Bureau (NBIB), an agency within the U.S. Office of Personnel Management (OPM). In 2019, the responsibility for carrying out background investigations transferred from OPM/NBIB to DoD, and specifically to DCSA. You may be familiar with these organizations from previous interactions with their investigators. Investigators who worked for OPM's NBIB were transferred to, and are now employees of, DCSA.

Question: Is DCSA a law enforcement or criminal justice agency?

Answer: No. DCSA is not a law enforcement or criminal justice agency as a matter of law—that is, its personnel do not have authority to carry firearms, make arrests, or administer criminal justice matters. However, under federal law, at 5 U.S.C. § 9101, DCSA is a "covered agency" authorized to collect CHRI from any law enforcement or criminal justice agency (for the purpose of conducting the background investigations of federal and U.S. military personnel). In other words, DCSA's background investigations and CHRI collection are an authorized law enforcement activity.

DCSA Investigators and the CHRI Request Process

Question: Who from DCSA requests CHRI, and whom do they request it from?

Answer: DCSA special agents, investigative assistants, and investigative specialists, as well as DCSA contract investigators, request CHRI from state, local, tribal, and territorial criminal justice and law enforcement departments or agencies while conducting background investigations for federal positions.

Question: How do DCSA personnel and contract investigators go about requesting CHRI?

Answer: DCSA requests CHRI from criminal justice and law enforcement departments or agencies through queries made by mail, email, phone, fax, and in-person visits. If one is available, investigators may also submit requests through an online portal service.

Question: What do these CHRI requests from DCSA look like?

Answer: DCSA mail, email, fax, and portal contacts typically have these characteristics:

- Mail: You will receive a form with the following nomenclature: INV FORM 44, "INVESTIGATIVE REQUEST FOR LAW ENFORCEMENT DATA." The text on this form is salmon/pink in color. It is also commonly referred to as an *inquiry* or *bubble sheet*.

- Email or fax: Investigators may also email or fax you with a request for CHRI for a particular subject, briefly explaining that the subject is a candidate for federal employment or military service. A release form may be attached to the email (or you may request that a release be provided), along with the investigator's contact information, to include badge number, @.gov or @.mil email address, and instructions on how to verify the investigator's official position.
- Internet portal queries: If your department or agency offers an online portal service to request CHRI, investigators may also submit their requests through the portal. Typically, investigators will supply the same information as noted for email and fax requests if your portal allows such inputs.

Question: Our department/agency received a request from a special agent via email or fax, and another request from a different special agent (or contract investigator) via email or fax, but the forms looked different. How can I tell if a DCSA request for CHRI is legitimate?

Answer: If you have questions or concerns about the legitimacy of a specific investigator's request, you can call (888) 795-5673 or email dcsa.boyers.bi.mbx.investigator-verifications@mail.mil to confirm their identity and status with DCSA. Please provide the investigator's contact information and badge number when reaching out to these points of contact.

Question: How do I know that a DCSA investigator (federal or contract) who comes to my department/agency is legitimate?

Answer: You can verify the status and identity of a DCSA investigator by calling (888) 795-5673 or emailing dcsa.boyers.bi.mbx.investigator-verifications@mail.mil. Please provide the investigator's contact information and badge number when reaching out to these points of contact. (Note: federal DCSA investigators will carry a gold badge; DCSA contract investigators will carry a silver badge.)

Question: Can I request that DCSA investigators reaching out to my department/agency use a particular request method (such as fax, email, or department/agency internet portal) that is convenient for me?

Answer: Yes. DCSA investigators are happy to send requests for CHRI in a manner and using a method that is most convenient and efficient for your department/agency if it is possible to do so. Please feel free to work with DCSA investigators or their regional supervisors to establish a process that works best for your department/agency.

Question: My department/agency charges a fee to respond to certain CHRI requests. How does DCSA handle fee charges?

Answer: DCSA is authorized to pay up to $15 to fulfill a subject CHRI request. This payment can be arranged by the DCSA investigator. However, it is important to note that federal law (at 5 U.S.C. § 9101) requires that all state, local, tribal, and territorial criminal justice and law enforcement agencies "shall" provide DCSA with requested CHRI regardless of any fee charges or schedules.

Question: Which companies does DCSA contract with to conduct background investigation services (i.e., contract investigators)?

Answer: DCSA contracts with multiple companies at any given time to conduct background investigations, so the list of contractors may change from year to year. For example, as of 2021, the following contractors are authorized to collect CHRI on behalf of DCSA: Securitas, Prospecta, and CACI.

Sharing CHRI with DCSA

Question: What kind of information does DCSA need from our agency?

Answer: DCSA investigators will want to know whether the subject of the investigation has a criminal history record with your department/agency. The law defines CHRI very broadly. A criminal history record includes identifiable descriptions and notations of arrests, indictments, information(s), any formal criminal charges (and any related disposition), sentencing, correction supervision, and release records. So, for example, DCSA requires any CHRI related to the following:

- felonies
- misdemeanors
- juvenile offenses
- traffic offenses
- open arrests
- pending criminal charges
- nolle prosequis
- not guilty determinations
- dismissals
- parole or probation records
- expungements
- sealed records
- any other violations of law that may or may not have resulted in a conviction
- additional information regarding other activities that do not result in criminal records.

DCSA investigators will also require police reports and/or other records containing pertinent information about each offense (if not contained in the records listed above), including the date and place of the offense, statement of the actual charge, and circumstances related to the offense or related to any interactions with law enforcement not resulting in an arrest or disposition. Please note that alleged or suspected criminal activity is pertinent to obtaining a complete history of the subject's activities and determining whether an individual is eligible for a sensitive position or a position of trust in the federal government.

Question: I am not sure whether my state or local laws prohibit me from disclosing certain CHRI to DCSA. What should I do?

Answer: DCSA has broad legal authority to collect CHRI from state, local, tribal, and territorial criminal justice and law enforcement departments or agencies (see later section on authorities). To verify this, departments and agencies often request advice or an opinion from their state, county, or local attorney or state attorney general's office to confirm that DCSA's federal authorities supersede all state, local, tribal, and territorial laws regarding CHRI disclosures. DCSA investigators can provide your county attorney or state attorney general's office with the necessary legal information.

Question: Why is sharing CHRI with DCSA important?

Answer: Sharing CHRI with DCSA enhances national security and public safety by ensuring the trustworthiness of the federal government workforce. For example, the failure to properly vet a federal employee in the past resulted in deadly and tragic consequences.

SOURCE: Federal Bureau of Investigation.

In 2013, Aaron Alexis—a former Navy service member and federal contractor—shot and killed 12 people and wounded four others, including a police officer, at the Washington Navy Yard. Alexis had a clearance and a badge to access the Navy Yard based on a prior background investigation. That background investigation had turned up a 2004 arrest, but the criminal disposition showed that the charges had been dismissed. However, had the investigator been able to obtain the full arrest record (i.e., the full CHRI on Alexis), he would have discovered that the 2004 arrest involved the unlawful discharge (three times) of a handgun. This information would have likely resulted in a more detailed background investigation and, possibly, a mental health evaluation and/or the denial of access credentials to Alexis—steps that might have saved lives.

Question: My department/agency does not have sufficient staff or resources to respond to DCSA's request within 30 days. How have other departments/agencies handled this issue?

Answer: Departments/agencies that do not have sufficient staff to respond to DCSA CHRI requests in a timely manner frequently provide DCSA staff (investigators or investigative assistants) with access to their local CHRI database. DCSA personnel are authorized (and have sufficient clearances) to become users of local criminal justice and law enforcement databases. If your database manager requires certain trainings to be completed or other procedures to be followed, DCSA staff will ensure appropriate compliance.

Question: Because of the coronavirus disease 2019 (COVID-19), we may be unable to provide data in person, or we may have changed our request procedures to facilitate remote interactions. Is there another way to send CHRI to investigators?

Answer: Yes. DCSA investigators can facilitate the sending of CHRI via mail, fax, secure email, or secure file transfer (e.g., DoD SAFE). Depending on your department/agency database access rules, you may also allow access to an online portal for investigators to collect data securely (as in the answer to the previous question).

Question: What about juvenile or other protected or sealed information? Do we need to share that with DCSA?

Answer: Yes. As noted above (sharing CHRI with DCSA) and below (DCSA authorities), the law authorizes DCSA to request and collect CHRI related to juveniles and to sealed, expunged, or other protected proceedings. DCSA investigators are trained to abide by the legal and court-ordered restrictions and conditions that are associated with the collection and use of this type of CHRI.

DCSA's Authorities to Acquire CHRI

Question: What is DCSA's statutory authority to collect CHRI?

Answer: Federal law, regulations, and executive orders provide DCSA with broad authority to collect CHRI:

- Title 5 of the United States Code, Section 9101, Security Clearance Information Act, as amended, provides that federal, state, or local criminal justice agencies shall, upon request by DoD (and DCSA as part of DoD) and other identified federal agencies, make available all CHRI regarding individuals under investigation by DCSA for a security clearance, eligibility for employment in a sensitive position, basic suitability or fitness for federal or contract employment, suitability for a public trust position, accession or retention in the armed forces, and identity credentialing under Homeland Security Presidential Directive 12 (HSPD-12).

- Pursuant to and consistent with section 3001(c) of the Intelligence Reform and Terrorism Prevention Act of 2004 (50 U.S.C. 3341(c)), sections 925(a)(1) and (d)(2) of the National Defense Authorization Act for Fiscal Year

2018 (10 U.S.C. 1564 note), and Executive Order 13467, DCSA is designated as "the primary entity for conducting effective, efficient, and secure background investigations for the federal government."

- Executive Order 13467: Reforming Processes Related to Suitability for Government Employment, Fitness for Contractor Employees, and Eligibility for Access to Classified National Security Information (June 30, 2008), as amended. This executive order was extensively amended by Executive Order 13869, Transferring Responsibilities for Background Investigations to the DoD on April 24, 2019.
- Title 5, Code of Federal Regulations, Part 731, regarding the adjudication of suitability and fitness determinations for federal personnel and contractors.

Question: In addition to the legal authorities, do all subjects of DCSA investigations also sign an Authorization for Release of Information permitting DCSA to request and collect all their CHRI?

Answer: Yes. Applicants for federal, federal contractor, and U.S. military positions sign a Standard Form 86, Authorization for Release of Information, to further ensure that DCSA is able to collect all information necessary for a background check (including all CHRI described above).

Question: May we request a copy of the individual's signed Authorization for Release of Information?

Answer: Yes. If you receive a DCSA request for CHRI, you may ask for a copy of the individual's signed Authorization for Release of Information by indicating this on the written request, responding via fax, phone, or email, or by contacting DCSA directly at (724) 794-5612. If an investigator contacts you in person, you may request a copy of the Authorization for Release of Information directly from the investigator. By law, federal agencies are required to accept electronic signatures (Public Law 105-277, Title XVII).

CHRI Sharing Assistance

Question: Where can I find more outreach, educational, and training materials on the topic of sharing CHRI with DCSA?

Answer: Educational and training materials are designed to help you and your department or agency share CHRI more effectively and efficiently and may be obtained from DCSA's Law Enforcement Liaison Office at DCSA.Law-Enforcement-Liaison@mail.mil.

Question: My department/agency has difficulty responding to DCSA requests for CHRI due to resource constraints. Where can I receive assistance and funding to help with CHRI requests?

Answer: Grants that might be used to assist with CHRI requests are available from the federal government. These include the National Criminal History Improvement Program through the Bureau of Justice Statistics and the Federal Emergency Management Agency's Grant Program.

Whom to Contact

Question: Whom can I contact in DCSA with questions or concerns?

Answer: For general information or questions concerning DCSA, its mission, its relationship with law enforcement agencies, and ways to partner to facilitate access to records, or to request specific outreach or educational presentations or materials, contact our Law Enforcement Liaison Office:

DCSA Law Enforcement Liaison Office
(202) 606-1606
DCSA.Law-Enforcement-Liaison@mail.mil

U.S. Department of Defense
Defense Counterintelligence and Security Agency
Attn: Law Enforcement Liaison Office
1900 E Street, NW
Washington, DC 20415

For assistance with replying to DCSA investigative inquiries, fees or billing, address changes, contract investigator authorization to receive records, referrals to other police or sheriffs' departments, and requests to switch to statewide access, please contact our records outreach department:

Federal Investigative Records Enterprise (FIRE), Records Outreach
(724) 794-5612

U.S. Department of Defense
Defense Counterintelligence and Security Agency
Attn: Federal Investigative Records Enterprise
Records Outreach
P.O. Box 618
1137 Branchton Road
Boyers, PA 16018-0618

DEFENSE COUNTERINTELLIGENCE AND SECURITY AGENCY

Photo credit: djedzura/Getty Images/iStockphoto

April 2022

APPENDIX D

Fact Sheet

The fact sheet is a concise summary of critical DCSA and CHRI sharing points:

- DCSA's mission
- a description of background investigations
- explanation of what constitutes CHRI
- information regarding both DCSA federal and contract investigators
- the processes and procedures for CHRI collection
- DCSA authorities
- contact information.

The fact sheet is designed for meetings and conversations that DCSA personnel have with SLTT LEA personnel in various circumstances (introductions, in-person inquiries, seminar, conferences, etc.). It will serve to facilitate explanatory conversation and provide SLTT LEAs with a reference document for subsequent use.

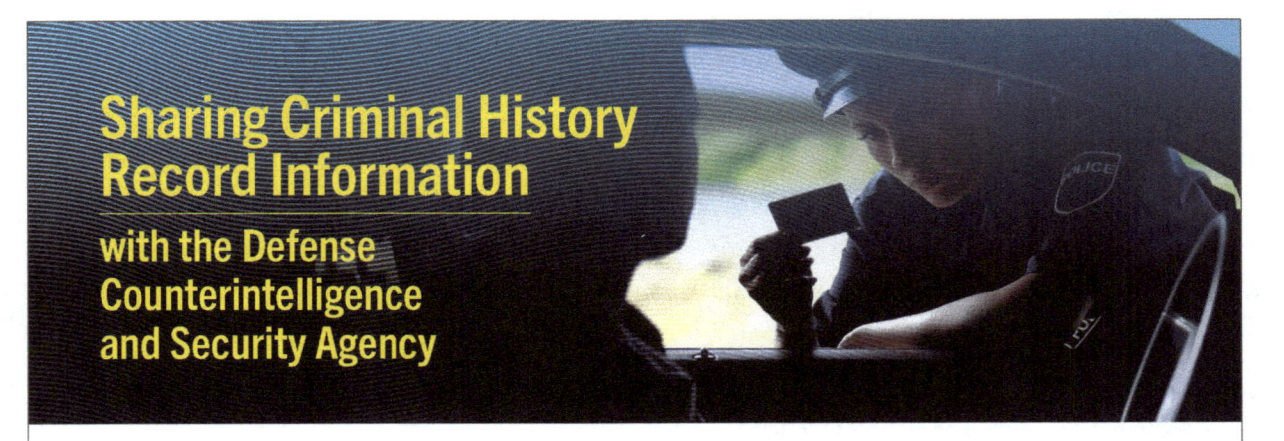

Sharing Criminal History Record Information with the Defense Counterintelligence and Security Agency

The U.S. Department of Defense's (DoD's) Defense Counterintelligence and Security Agency (DCSA) ensures the trustworthiness of federal workers and contractors. DCSA conducts background investigations as part of its personnel vetting program, one prong of a four-pronged approach to carrying out the agency's mission. One of the primary tools DCSA uses to vet personnel is the security clearance process, which requires criminal history record information (CHRI) from state, local, tribal, and territorial (SLTT) criminal justice and law enforcement agencies. The cooperation of SLTT criminal justice and law enforcement entities is key to the success of DCSA's personnel vetting enterprise, which is a critical component of national security.

DCSA's Mission

Through vetting, industry engagement, counterintelligence support, and education, secure the trustworthiness of the U.S. government's workforce, the integrity of its cleared contractor support, and the uncompromised nature of its technologies, services, and supply chains.

DCSA and Background Investigations (Personnel Vetting)

- In 2019, DCSA assumed responsibility for the federal government's personnel vetting mission from the Office of Personnel Management (OPM). Many OPM investigators and other personnel transferred to DCSA and are now a vital part of its organization.
- Federal departments, agencies, offices, and the U.S. military use DCSA investigations to determine an individual's suitability and eligibility for employment, ability to hold sensitive positions, and access to federal facilities, automated systems, or classified information.
- DCSA supports over 100 federal entities and conducts over 2 million background investigations per year—approximately 95 percent of all federal background investigations.

DCSA's Criminal History Record Information Needs

- CHRI is an important input to background investigations. DCSA's work with SLTT criminal justice and law enforcement partners to request and acquire CHRI is an essential part of the background investigation process. Quickly responding to these requests allows DCSA to process security clearances rapidly and accurately.
- CHRI includes the following:
  - identifiable descriptions and notations of arrests, indictments, interactions, or
  - other formal criminal charges, and
  - any disposition arising from the above, or
  - any sentencing, correction supervision, and release information
  - sealed records that are accessible by state and local criminal justice agencies for the purpose of conducting background checks.
- When DCSA investigators request CHRI from a criminal justice or law enforcement agency, they need
  - to know whether the subject of the investigation has a criminal history record with your agency or department
  - any criminal record associated with the subject, to include felonies, misdemeanors, traffic offenses, or any other violations of law that may or may not have resulted in a conviction
  - pertinent information about each offense, including the date and place of the offense, statement of the actual charge, circumstances related to the offense, and its disposition
  - copies of relevant police reports or other similar records of interaction with your agency or department. This information may also include

records of alleged or suspected criminal activity of a subject. Such records are part of the complete history of the subject's activities and are required to assess the suitability of an individual to hold sensitive federal positions or access sensitive or classified information.

Who Will Contact You from DCSA

- *DCSA federal personnel*: Special Agents-in-Charge, Special Agents, Investigative Assistants, Investigative Specialists, and other DCSA support staff.
- *DCSA contract investigators*: Federal law, specifically 5 U.S.C. § 9101(6)(J), authorizes DoD to employ contract investigators to support DCSA background investigation activities and operations. Therefore, DCSA contract investigators have the same authority as DCSA federal investigators to collect CHRI.

On every introduction, DCSA personnel and contract investigators will present credentials and badges (gold for federal investigators, silver for contract investigators) in person or will provide a badge number (by phone, fax, or electronic means) identifying them as DCSA representatives. Upon request, they will also share the individual subject's signed Authorization for Release of Information. You may verify their identity, position, and authority by contacting DCSA using the information provided at the end of this sheet.

How DCSA Requests CHRI

- DCSA mails an investigative request form (INV FORM 44, "INVESTIGATIVE REQUEST FOR LAW ENFORCEMENT DATA") to criminal justice and law enforcement agencies to request a subject's CHRI. This form is also commonly referred to as an *inquiry* or *bubble sheet*.
- If DCSA does not receive a completed investigative request form and accompanying records information, DCSA investigators and contractors will conduct investigative checks to acquire the necessary information. DCSA agents and contractors often conduct these checks in person, but they may also be conducted via phone, fax, email, or internet portal.

Why DCSA Is Permitted to Collect This Information

As an element of DoD, DCSA derives its authority to conduct background investigations from U.S. laws, executive orders, federal regulations, and delegations, including but not limited to the following:

- *Title 5 of the U.S.C. § 9101, Security Clearance Information Act*
  - This law provides that federal, state, or local criminal justice agencies will, upon request by DoD and other identified federal agencies (such as DCSA and its contractors), make available all criminal history record information regarding individuals under investigation by DoD for
    » a security clearance
    » eligibility for employment in a sensitive position
    » basic suitability or fitness for federal or contract employment
    » suitability for a public trust position, accession or retention in the armed forces
    » identity credentialing under Homeland Security Presidential Directive 12 (HSPD-12).
- *Executive Order 13467: Reforming Processes Related to Suitability for Government Employment, Fitness for Contractor Employees, and Eligibility for Access to Classified National Security Information (June 30, 2008)*
  - This executive order designated DCSA as "the primary entity for conducting effective, efficient, and secure background investigations for the federal government."
  - This executive order directed the transfer of the investigative functions, resources, and personnel of the OPM's National Background Investigations Bureau (NBIB) to DCSA.

DCSA Contact Information

For questions related to an agent or investigator's identity, position, and authority, contact the DCSA Safety and Security Team at (888) 795-5673, Monday through Friday, 7 a.m.–4 p.m. ET.

For questions about DCSA and its partnership with law enforcement agencies, please contact the DCSA Law Enforcement Liaison Office at (202) 606-1606 or DCSA.Law-Enforcement-Liaison@mail.mil.

For assistance with completing investigative request forms, please contact DCSA Records Outreach at (724) 794-5612.

DEFENSE COUNTERINTELLIGENCE AND SECURITY AGENCY

Photo credit: Motortion/Getty Images/iStockphoto

April 2022

APPENDIX E

One-Pagers

The one-pagers are brief distillations of DCSA as an organization, its authorities, the purpose of background investigations, DCSA staff and contractors whom SLTT LEAs will interact with, CHRI definition and types, and why CHRI sharing is important for national security and public safety. Each one-pager is formatted differently and includes different levels of detail. The substance and layout of the one-pagers are designed for the rapid distribution and explanation of DCSA's CHRI sharing needs in circumstances under which the amount of time with SLTT LEA personnel is very limited (e.g., an in-person law check, an email or fax contact or introduction, or brief interactions at seminar or conference booths).

One-Pager 1

Sharing Criminal History Record Information with DCSA

The Defense Counterintelligence and Security Agency (DCSA) is an agency within the U.S. Department of Defense that is dedicated to protecting America's trusted workforce and workspaces—physical or virtual. DCSA joins two essential missions: personnel vetting and critical technology protection, supported by counterintelligence and training, education, and certification functions.

DCSA's Representatives

- *DCSA federal personnel:* Special Agents-in-Charge, Special Agents, Investigative Assistants, Investigative Specialists, and other DCSA support staff.
- *DCSA contract investigators:* DCSA contracts with multiple private companies to assist in conducting background investigations. Federal law provides DCSA's contractors with the same authority as federal investigators and staff to obtain criminal history record information (CHRI) from federal, state, local, territorial, tribal, and other criminal justice agencies.

What DCSA Needs from Criminal Justice Agencies

- DCSA requires CHRI to conduct background investigations and vetting on individuals applying for federal government sensitive, nonsensitive, and national security positions.
- The investigator will need to know whether you have CHRI on the subject and, if so, they will need all criminal history records, information about each offense, and copies of any relevant police reports.

What is CHRI?

Under federal law, the term *criminal history record information* means any information collected by criminal justice agencies on individuals, consisting of identifiable descriptions and notations of arrests, indictments, information(s), any formal criminal charges (and any related disposition), sentencing, correction supervision, and release records. This definition includes information about ANY criminal activity, even if there is no arrest or court disposition.

Why You Are Authorized to Release CHRI to DCSA

- DCSA is authorized by federal law (i.e., 5 U.S.C. § 9101) to receive CHRI from criminal justice agencies, such as your organization, for the purpose of conducting background investigations.
- This federal law supersedes all state and local laws that otherwise restrict CHRI release. Criminal justice agencies are not liable for the information that they share with DCSA.

The Importance of Sharing Information with DCSA

It is critical to share information with DCSA because it is required by law (for all federal, state, local, territorial, and tribal entities), enhances national security and public safety, and ensures a trusted federal workforce.

DEFENSE COUNTERINTELLIGENCE AND SECURITY AGENCY

Photo credit: fstop123/Getty Images/iStockphoto

April 2022

One-Pager 2

Collaborating with DCSA to Ensure Public Safety and National Security

Who is DCSA?

The Defense Counterintelligence and Security Agency (DCSA) is an agency within the U.S. Department of Defense. DCSA is the security agency in the federal government dedicated to protecting America's trusted workforce and trusted workspaces—whether physical or virtual. DCSA is a critical component to the nation's national security.

What Does DCSA Do?

A part of DCSA's mission involves vetting personnel for trusted positions in the U.S. Department of Defense. As part of the vetting mission, DCSA conducts security, suitability, and fitness background investigations for access to classified information and nonsensitive positions for over two million federal employees, federal contractors, and U.S. military personnel each year. DCSA investigators and DCSA's contract investigators collect criminal history record information (CHRI) as part of these investigations and vetting processes.

What Does DCSA Need from Your Criminal Justice or Law Enforcement Agency?

DCSA uses CHRI in conducting background investigations and vetting on individuals applying for federal government sensitive, nonsensitive, and national security positions. The DCSA investigator will need to know if you have CHRI on the subject and, if so, they will need all criminal history records, information about each offense, and copies of any relevant police reports.

What is CHRI?

Under federal law, the term *criminal history record information* means any information collected by criminal justice agencies on individuals consisting of identifiable descriptions and notations of arrests, indictments, information(s), any formal criminal charges (and any related disposition), sentencing, correction supervision, and release records. This definition includes information about ANY criminal activity, even if there is no arrest or court disposition.

Why Are You Authorized to Release CHRI to DCSA?

DCSA is authorized by federal law (i.e., 5 U.S.C. § 9101) to receive CHRI from any criminal justice or law enforcement agency. This federal law supersedes all state and local laws that otherwise restrict CHRI release. Criminal justice agencies are not liable for the CHRI that they share with DCSA.

Who Are DCSA's Investigators Collecting CHRI from Your Department/Agency?

DCSA federal personnel: Special Agents-in-Charge, Special Agents, Investigative Assistants, Investigative Specialists, and other DCSA support staff.

DCSA contract investigators: DCSA contracts with multiple private companies (Securitas, Prospecta, and CACI, as of 2021) to assist in conducting background investigations. Federal law provides that DCSA's contractors have the same authority as federal investigators and staff to obtain CHRI.

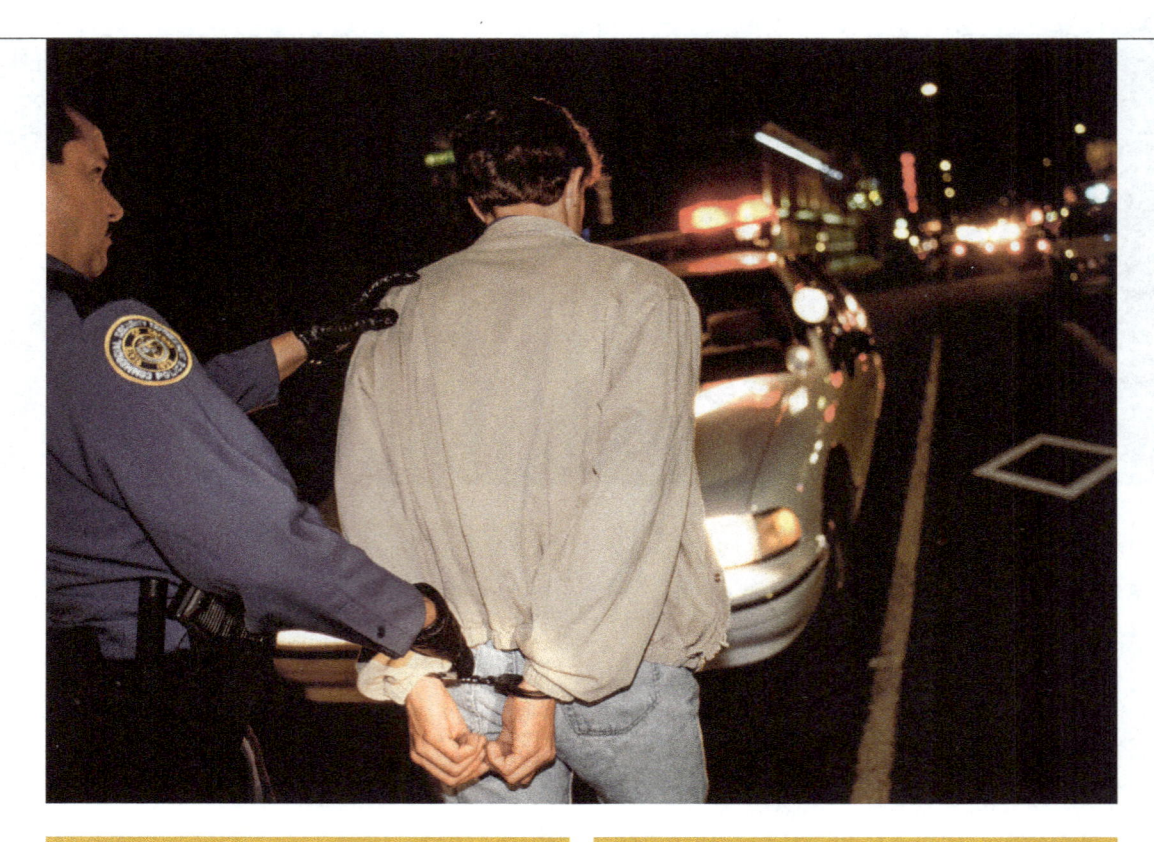

Why Is It Important to Share Information with DCSA?

It is critical to share information with DCSA because it is required by law (for all federal, state, local, territorial, and tribal entities), enhances national security and public safety, and ensures a trusted federal workforce.

Whom Should You Contact Within DCSA If You Have Questions?

For questions about DCSA, its mission, its relationship with law enforcement agencies, and ways to partner to facilitate access to records, or to request specific outreach or educational presentations or materials, **contact the DCSA Law Enforcement Liaison Office at (202) 606-1606,** DCSA.Law-Enforcement-Liaison@mail.mil.

For assistance with replying to DCSA investigative inquiries, fees/billing, address changes, contract agent authorization to receive records, referrals to other police departments, or requesting to switch to statewide access, please contact the **Federal Investigative Records Enterprise (FIRE), Records Outreach, at (724) 794-5612.**

DEFENSE COUNTERINTELLIGENCE AND SECURITY AGENCY

Photo credit: fstop123/Getty Images/iStockphoto

April 2022

One-Pager 3

DCSA CHRI Sharing 101
Defense Counterintelligence and Security Agency

The Defense Counterintelligence and Security Agency (DCSA) is an agency within the Department of Defense dedicated to protecting America's trusted workforce and workspaces—physical or virtual.

WHO?

Mission
DCSA combines two essential missions: personnel vetting and critical technology protection, supported by counterintelligence and training, education, and certification functions.

Service
DCSA serves over 100 federal entities, oversees 10,000 cleared companies, and conducts over 2 million background investigations each year.

Formerly known as
National Background Investigations Bureau (NBIB), an agency of the United States Office of Personnel Management

WHAT?

DCSA conducts background investigations to determine
- suitability for government employment
- fitness for an appointment to a service position and/or to perform work under a government contract
- eligibility to serve in a national security sensitive position
- acceptance or retention in the armed forces
- eligibility for access to classified information, and/or for technological/physical access to a federally controlled facility or information technology system.

DCSA representatives
- **DCSA federal personnel:** Investigative Special Agents, specialists, assistants, and other staff
- **DCSA contract investigators:** Federal law provides that contractors have the same authority as federal investigators and staff to obtain criminal history record information (CHRI) from federal, state, local, territorial, tribal, and other criminal justice agencies.

HOW?

Obtaining CHRI
For national security vetting purposes, the investigator will need all criminal history record(s) related to

- felonies
- misdemeanors
- juvenile offenses
- traffic offenses
- open arrests
- pending criminal charges
- nolle prosequis
- not guilty determinations
- dismissals
- expungements
- sealed records
- copies of any police reports or similar information
- any other violations of law that may or may not have resulted in a conviction.

WHY?

It is important to share criminal history information with DCSA
- required by law (for all federal, state, local, territorial, and tribal entities)
- enhances national security
- enhances public safety
- ensures a trusted federal workforce.

Need More Information? Contact the DCSA Law Enforcement Liaison Office by phone, (202) 606-1606, or email: DCSA.Law-Enforcement-Liaison@mail.mil

Photo credit: Aldeca Productions - stock.adobe.com

April 2022

APPENDIX F

Brochures

The two brochures reconceive the current DCSA brochure. They are informational documents that cover all major points from the *CHRI Sharing Guidebook* (i.e., DCSA as an organization, DCSA authorities, CHRI collection processes and procedures, what constitutes CHRI, and how CHRI sharing can be made easier), but in a bullet-point and short-sentence style. The redesign and creation of two shorter brochures reflects the feedback that the RAND team received regarding the current brochure—i.e., that it is too long and densely worded for many interactions with SLTT LEA personnel. The redesigns are an effort to provide materials suitable for broad distribution among SLTT LEA jurisdictions and give DCSA field staff a "leave-behind" that is both comprehensive and easy to digest.

Brochure 7 x 9

Sharing Criminal History Record Information with DCSA

DEFENSE COUNTERINTELLIGENCE AND SECURITY AGENCY

What is DCSA?

DCSA is the Defense Counterintelligence and Security Agency—an agency within the U.S. Department of Defense. Federal departments, agencies, offices, and the U.S. military use DCSA investigations to determine an individual's suitability and eligibility for employment, ability to hold sensitive positions, and access to federal facilities, automated systems, or classified information.

Whom you will interact with from DCSA

- **DCSA personnel:** Special Agents-in-Charge, Special Agents, Investigative Assistants, Investigative Specialists and other DCSA support staff.
- **DCSA contract investigators:** Federal law, specifically 5 U.S.C. § 9101(6)(J), authorizes the Department of Defense to employ contract investigators to support DCSA background investigation activities and operations. DCSA contract investigators have the same authority to collect criminal history record information (CHRI) as DCSA federal investigators.

Upon every introduction, DCSA special agents and contract investigators will present credentials and badges (gold for federal investigators, silver for contract investigators) identifying them as DCSA representatives. You may verify their identity, position, and authority by contacting DCSA using the information provided below. However, current regulations prohibit photocopies of investigator credentials.

Investigators may also provide you with an Authorization for Release of Information form signed by the subject of the background investigation.

For questions related to an agent or investigator's identity, position, and authority, contact the DCSA Safety and Security Team at (888) 795-5673, Monday through Friday, 7 a.m.–4 p.m. ET.

What DCSA needs from you

- The investigator will want to know whether the subject of the investigation has a criminal history record with your department.
- A criminal history record includes felonies, misdemeanors, traffic offenses, or other violations of law that may or may not have resulted in a conviction.
- The investigator may request pertinent information about each offense, including the date and place of the offense, statement of the actual charge, circumstances related to the offense, and its disposition. In addition, the investigator may ask for a copy of the police report. DCSA may also require additional information regarding other activities that do not result in criminal records. Please note that records of alleged or suspected criminal activity are part of a subject's complete history and are required to assess the suitability to hold sensitive federal positions or access sensitive information.

Defining CHRI for national security vetting purposes

- Under federal law, at 5 U.S.C. § 9101(a)(2), the term *criminal history record information* means information collected on individuals by criminal justice agencies consisting of identifiable descriptions and notations of arrests, indictments, information, or other formal criminal charges, and any disposition arising therefrom, sentencing, correction supervision, and release records. The term does not include identification information, such as fingerprint records, to the extent that such information does not indicate involvement of the individual in the criminal justice system. The term includes those records of a state or locality sealed pursuant to law if such records are accessible by state and local criminal justice agencies for the purpose of conducting background checks.

Why it is important to share CHRI with DCSA

- Sharing CHRI helps ensure national security and public safety through vetting people's backgrounds and ensuring that they meet the sensitive needs of the positions for which they are applying.
- It is required by law (for all federal, state, local, territorial, and tribal entities) under 5 U.S.C. § 9101(b).
- It provides the federal government with a trusted federal workforce. Just as state, local, territorial, and tribal law enforcement agencies require criminal history record information for their sworn and non-sworn personnel to ensure a trustworthy workforce, so do positions in the U.S. military and federal departments, agencies, and offices.

How you'll interact with DCSA

- **Investigative request standardized forms:** DCSA sends standardized inquiry forms requesting CHRI via mail. These written requests are sometimes referred to as *inquiry* or *bubble sheets*.
- **Investigator checks:** DCSA or contract investigators directly request CHRI using the law enforcement agency's preferred methods, if known. These requests are typically made in writing by a Special Agent or contract investigator, via fax, email, in-person visit, over the phone, or through an internet portal. These requests are sometimes referred to as *law checks*. You may work with the local field office to determine the most efficient way to provide information to DCSA.

DCSA authorities

As an office within the U.S. Department of Defense, DCSA derives its authority to conduct background investigations from U.S. laws, executive orders, federal regulations, and delegations, including but not limited to the following:

- **Title 5 U.S.C. § 9101 Security Clearance Information Act, as amended:** This federal law states that federal, state, or local criminal justice agencies will, upon request by the Department of Defense and other identified federal agencies [such as DCSA and its contractors], make available all CHRI regarding individuals under investigation by the Department of Defense for a security clearance.
- **Executive Order 13467: Reforming Processes Related to Suitability for Government Employment, Fitness for Contractor Employees, and Eligibility for Access to Classified National Security Information (June 30, 2008), as amended:** This executive order designates DCSA as "the primary entity for conducting effective, efficient, and secure background investigations for the federal government."

The executive order also directed the transfer of the investigative functions, resources, and personnel of the Office of Personnel Management's (OPM's) National Background Investigations Bureau (NBIB) to DCSA.

DCSA contact information

For more questions about DCSA, its mission, its relationship with law enforcement agencies, ways to partner to facilitate access to records, or to request specific outreach or educational presentation or materials, contact

DCSA Law Enforcement Liaison Office
(202) 606-1606
DCSA.Law-Enforcement-Liaison@mail.mil

U.S. Department of Defense
Defense Counterintelligence and Security Agency
Attn: Law Enforcement Liaison Office
1900 E Street, NW
Washington, DC 20415

For assistance with replying to DCSA investigative inquiries, fees/billing, address changes, contract agent authorization to receive records, referrals to other police departments, and requests to switch to statewide access, please contact

Federal Investigative Records Enterprise (FIRE), Records Outreach
(724) 794-5612

U.S. Department of Defense
Defense Counterintelligence and Security Agency
Attn: Federal Investigative Records Enterprise, Records Outreach
P.O. Box 618
1137 Branchton Road
Boyers, PA 16018-0618

DEFENSE COUNTERINTELLIGENCE AND SECURITY AGENCY

Photo credits: kali9/Getty Images/iStockphoto

April 2022

Brochure Trifold

Why it is important to share information with DCSA

- enhances national security
- enhances public safety
- required by law (for all federal, state, local, territorial, and tribal entities)

Your information-sharing cooperation also helps to ensure a trusted federal workforce.

Just as state, local, territorial, and tribal law enforcement agencies require criminal history information for their sworn and non-sworn personnel to ensure a trustworthy workforce, so do positions in the U.S. military and federal departments, agencies, and offices.

Contact information

For more questions about DCSA, its mission, its relationship with law enforcement agencies, ways to partner to facilitate access to records, or to request specific outreach or educational presentations or materials, contact

DCSA Law Enforcement Liaison Office
Phone: (202) 606-1606
Email: DCSA.Law-Enforcement-Liaison@mail.mil
Mail: U.S. Department of Defense
Defense Counterintelligence and Security Agency
Attn: Law Enforcement Liaison Office
1900 E Street, NW
Washington, DC 20415

For assistance with replying to DCSA investigative inquiries, fees/billing, address changes, contract investigator authorization to receive records, referrals to other police departments, and requests to switch to statewide access, please contact

Federal Investigative Records Enterprise (FIRE), Records Outreach
Phone: (724) 794-5612
Mail: U.S. Department of Defense
Defense Counterintelligence and Security Agency
Attn: Federal Investigative Records Enterprise, Records Outreach
P.O. Box 618
1137 Branchton Road
Boyers, PA 16018-0618

DEFENSE COUNTERINTELLIGENCE AND SECURITY AGENCY

Photo credits: Cover: RyanJLane/Getty Images;
interior: kali9/Getty Images/iStockphoto;
back cover: KatarzynaBialasiewicz/Getty Images/iStockphoto   April 2022

Criminal Justice and the U.S. Department of Defense

DEFENSE COUNTERINTELLIGENCE AND SECURITY AGENCY

You have received an inquiry (mail, email, fax, phone) or been approached by a DCSA federal investigator or contract investigator for criminal history record information.
Here is how you can help our national security efforts.

Our mission

Federal departments, agencies, offices, and the U.S. military use Defense Counterintelligence and Security Agency (DCSA) investigations to determine an individual's suitability and eligibility for employment, ability to hold sensitive positions, and access to federal facilities, automated systems, or classified information.

DCSA authorities

As an agency of the Department of Defense, DCSA derives its authority to conduct background investigations from U.S. laws, executive orders, federal regulations, and delegations, including but not limited to the following:

- Title 5 of the United States Code § 9101, Security Clearance Information Act
- Executive Order 13467: Reforming Processes Related to Suitability for Government Employment, Fitness for Contractor Employees, and Eligibility for Access to Classified National Security Information (June 30, 2008).

Whom you will interact with from DCSA

- *DCSA federal personnel*: Investigative Special Agents, specialists, assistants, and other staff
- *DCSA contract investigators*: Federal law provides to contractors the same authority as federal special agents and staff to obtain criminal history record information (CHRI).

What our agents and investigators will provide

- Credentials and badges identifying themselves as DCSA representatives
- Individual subject's signed Authorization for Release of Information (to DCSA), if requested
- DCSA contact information.

For questions related to an agent or investigator's identity, position, and authority, contact the DCSA Safety and Security Team at (888) 795-5673, Monday through Friday, 7 a.m.–4 p.m. ET.

How DCSA will request records

- Investigative request forms: DCSA sends standardized inquiry forms requesting CHRI via the U.S. Postal Service
- Investigator checks: DCSA or contract investigators directly request CHRI using the law enforcement agency's preferred method, if known. Requests are typically made in-person but may also be made via writing, phone, fax, email, or an internet portal.

What DCSA needs from you

We are seeking CHRI for national security vetting purposes. The investigator will need to ask:

- Does the subject of the investigation have a criminal history record with your department, agency, or office?

If yes, the investigator may need the following:

- all criminal history record(s), including felonies, misdemeanors, traffic offenses, or other violations of law that may or may not have resulted in a conviction
- information about each offense, including the date and place of the offense, statement of the actual charge, circumstances related to the offense, and its disposition
- copies of any police report(s). Please note that records of alleged or suspected criminal activity of a subject are required to assess the suitability of an individual to hold sensitive federal positions or access sensitive information.

The federal statutory definition of CHRI

The term *criminal history record information* means information collected by criminal justice agencies on individuals consisting of the following:

- identifiable descriptions and notations of arrests, indictments, information, or
- other formal criminal charges, and
- any disposition arising from the above, or
- any sentencing, correction supervision, and release information.

The term includes those records of a state or locality sealed pursuant to law if such records are accessible by state and local criminal justice agencies for the purpose of conducting background checks.

APPENDIX G
Email

The email is designed as a first introduction of DCSA to SLTT LEA personnel, should DCSA staff decide to reach out by email to initiate SLTT relationships and partnerships. The email can be personalized (if needed) to particular personnel or POCs, such as a police chief, records manager, or dispatch supervisor. It offers a short summary of DCSA's mission, its need for CHRI, and a brief description of the suite of education and training materials developed through this project. The primary goal of the email is to provide SLTT LEA POCs with the opportunity to quickly and efficiently forward and disseminate key information and supporting materials about DCSA and CHRI to their own staff by electronic means.

Dear [Addressee],

The U.S. Department of Defense's Defense Counterintelligence and Security Agency (DCSA) helps to preserve national security by ensuring the trustworthiness of the federal workforce and workspaces. The agency accomplishes this work through personnel vetting, critical technology protection, and counterintelligence training, education, and certification.

As part of DCSA's personnel vetting program, the agency conducts background investigations for individuals seeking to hold federal positions and access sensitive information. In doing so, DCSA relies on the cooperation of state, local, territorial, and tribal law enforcement and criminal justice agencies to share relevant criminal history record information (CHRI). Your agency helps DCSA meet its mission to ensure the trustworthiness of those individuals who serve in the federal government and U.S. military.

To better facilitate the cooperation between DCSA and your agency, we developed multiple training tools and outreach materials on DCSA, its background investigation mission, why it is important to share CHRI with DCSA, and how to share CHRI with DCSA. These tools and materials should provide the information you and your personnel need to partner with DCSA to help preserve national security.

If you have questions about these resources, sharing CHRI with DCSA, or how you can further support DCSA's national security mission, please contact DCSA's Law Enforcement Liaison Office by phone—(202) 606-1606—or email: DCSA.Law-Enforcement-Liaison@mail.mil.

Sincerely,
DCSA Law Enforcement Liaison

DEFENSE COUNTERINTELLIGENCE AND SECURITY AGENCY

Photo credit: Motortion/Getty Images/iStockphoto

April 2022

APPENDIX H

Training Presentation

The training presentation revises and consolidates DCSA's current (and detailed) training presentations used to brief agency field staff and SLTT LEA personnel. The presentation is designed to be accessible and digestible for a broader SLTT LEA audience (i.e., SLTT leaders, mangers, or staff—from police chiefs to records or dispatch clerks). Additionally, the presentation incorporates more visual components to maintain audience interest, and the slides are constructed to deliver critical points more quickly (i.e., DCSA as an organization, DCSA authorities, CHRI collection processes and procedures, what constitutes CHRI, and how CHRI sharing can be made easier) for interactions with SLTT LEA personnel that are more time-limited (e.g., ad hoc training briefs, conferences, or seminars where DCSA is an invitee or attendee).

AGENDA

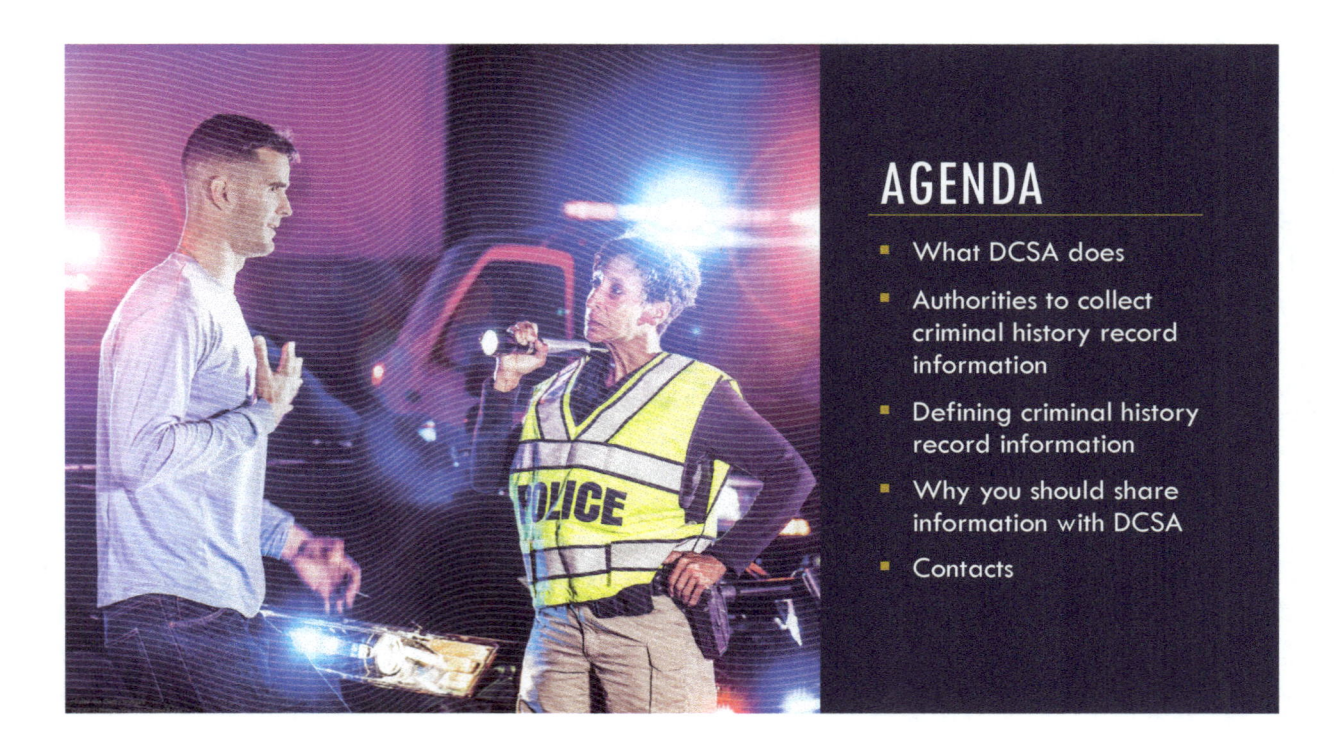

- What DCSA does
- Authorities to collect criminal history record information
- Defining criminal history record information
- Why you should share information with DCSA
- Contacts

WHAT DCSA DOES

DCSA PROTECTS THE NATION'S WORKFORCE AND WORKSPACES

- Vet personnel
- Critical technology protection

DCSA & BACKGROUND INVESTIGATIONS

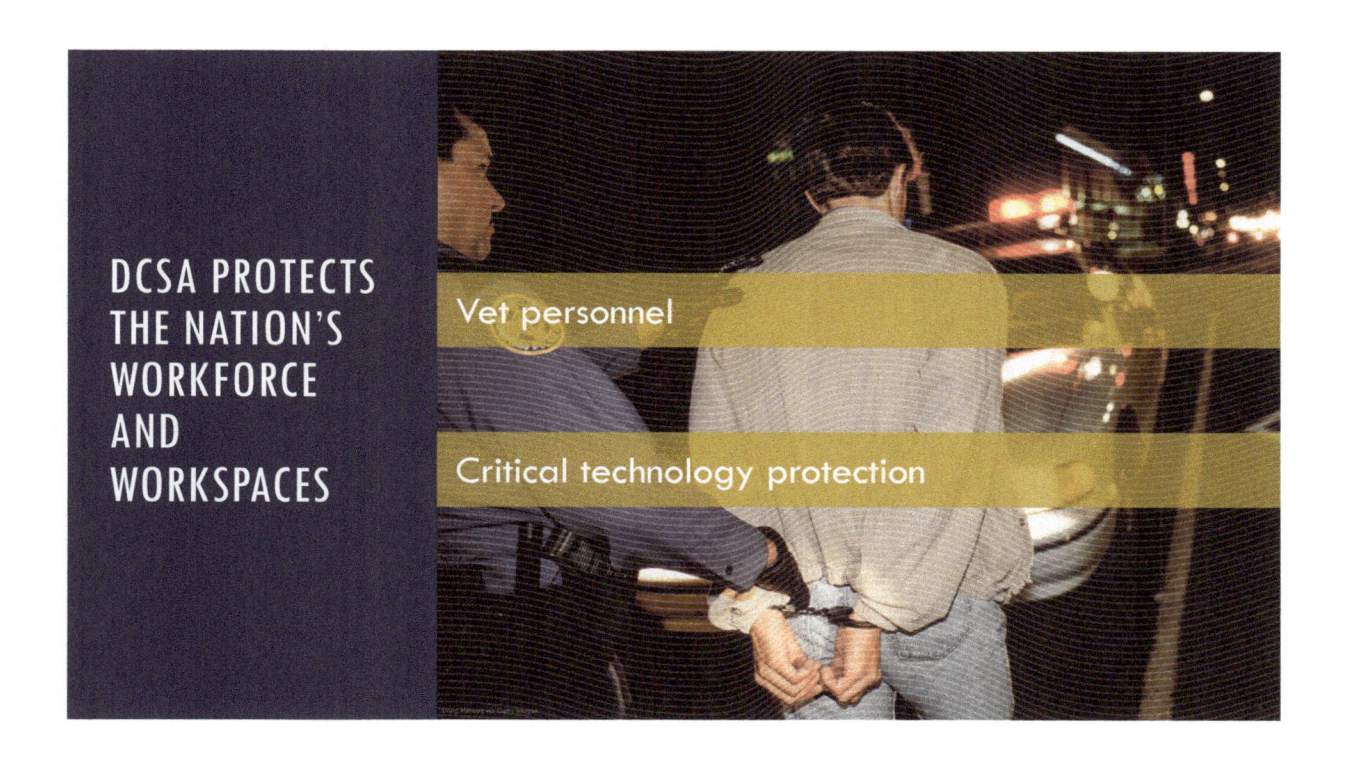

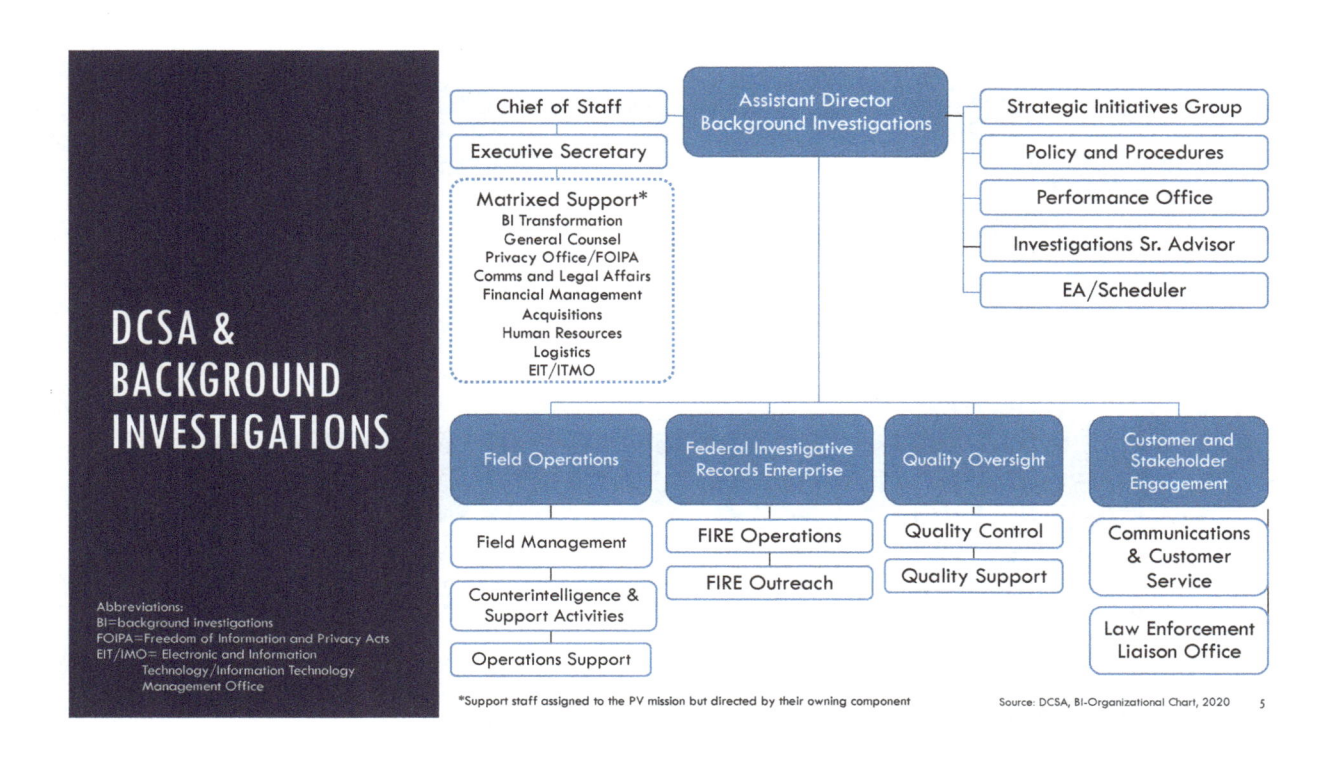

Abbreviations:
BI=background investigations
FOIPA=Freedom of Information and Privacy Acts
EIT/IMO= Electronic and Information Technology/Information Technology Management Office

Organizational chart:

- **Assistant Director Background Investigations**
  - Chief of Staff
  - Executive Secretary
  - Matrixed Support*
    - BI Transformation
    - General Counsel
    - Privacy Office/FOIPA
    - Comms and Legal Affairs
    - Financial Management
    - Acquisitions
    - Human Resources
    - Logistics
    - EIT/ITMO
  - Strategic Initiatives Group
  - Policy and Procedures
  - Performance Office
  - Investigations Sr. Advisor
  - EA/Scheduler

- **Field Operations**
  - Field Management
  - Counterintelligence & Support Activities
  - Operations Support

- **Federal Investigative Records Enterprise**
  - FIRE Operations
  - FIRE Outreach

- **Quality Oversight**
  - Quality Control
  - Quality Support

- **Customer and Stakeholder Engagement**
  - Communications & Customer Service
  - Law Enforcement Liaison Office

*Support staff assigned to the PV mission but directed by their owning component

Source: DCSA, BI-Organizational Chart, 2020

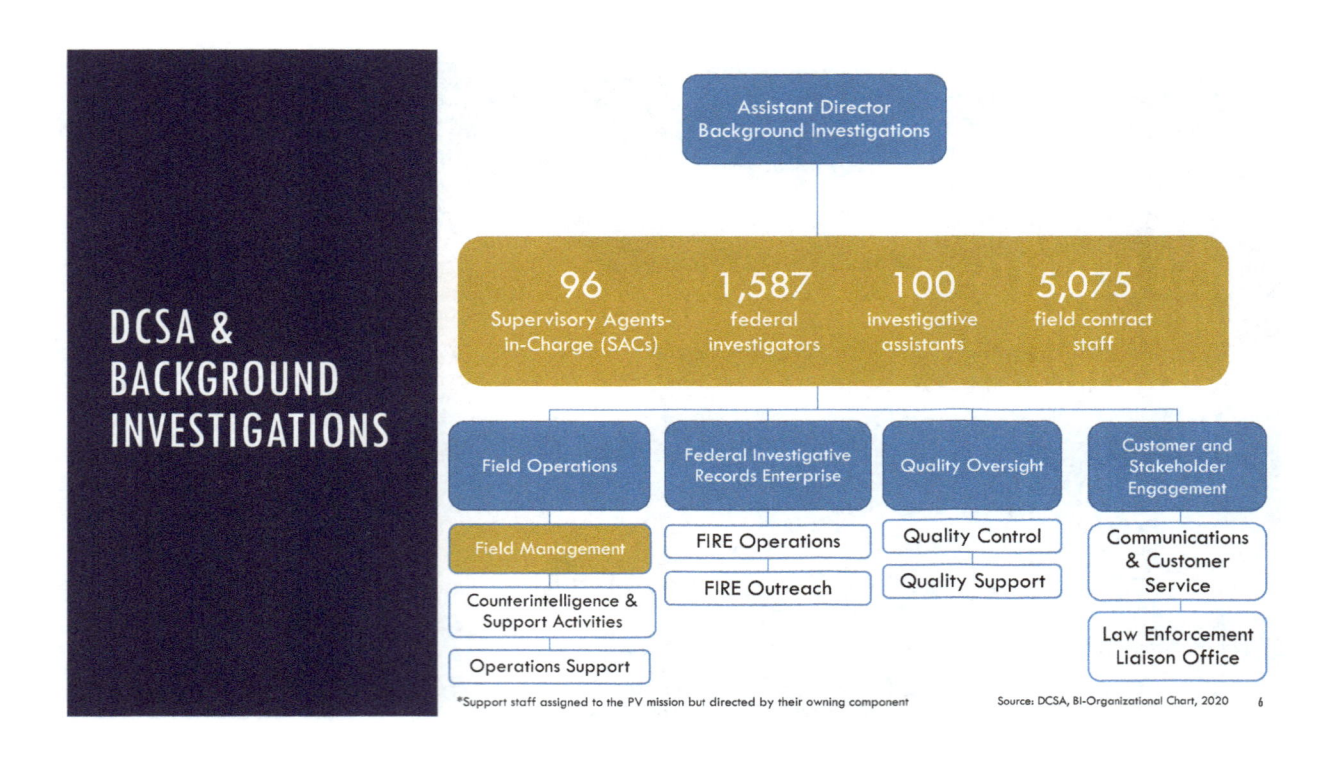

DCSA & BACKGROUND INVESTIGATIONS

Assistant Director Background Investigations

- **96** Supervisory Agents-in-Charge (SACs)
- **1,587** federal investigators
- **100** investigative assistants
- **5,075** field contract staff

- Field Operations
  - Field Management
  - Counterintelligence & Support Activities
  - Operations Support
- Federal Investigative Records Enterprise
  - FIRE Operations
  - FIRE Outreach
- Quality Oversight
  - Quality Control
  - Quality Support
- Customer and Stakeholder Engagement
  - Communications & Customer Service
  - Law Enforcement Liaison Office

*Support staff assigned to the PV mission but directed by their owning component

Source: DCSA, BI-Organizational Chart, 2020

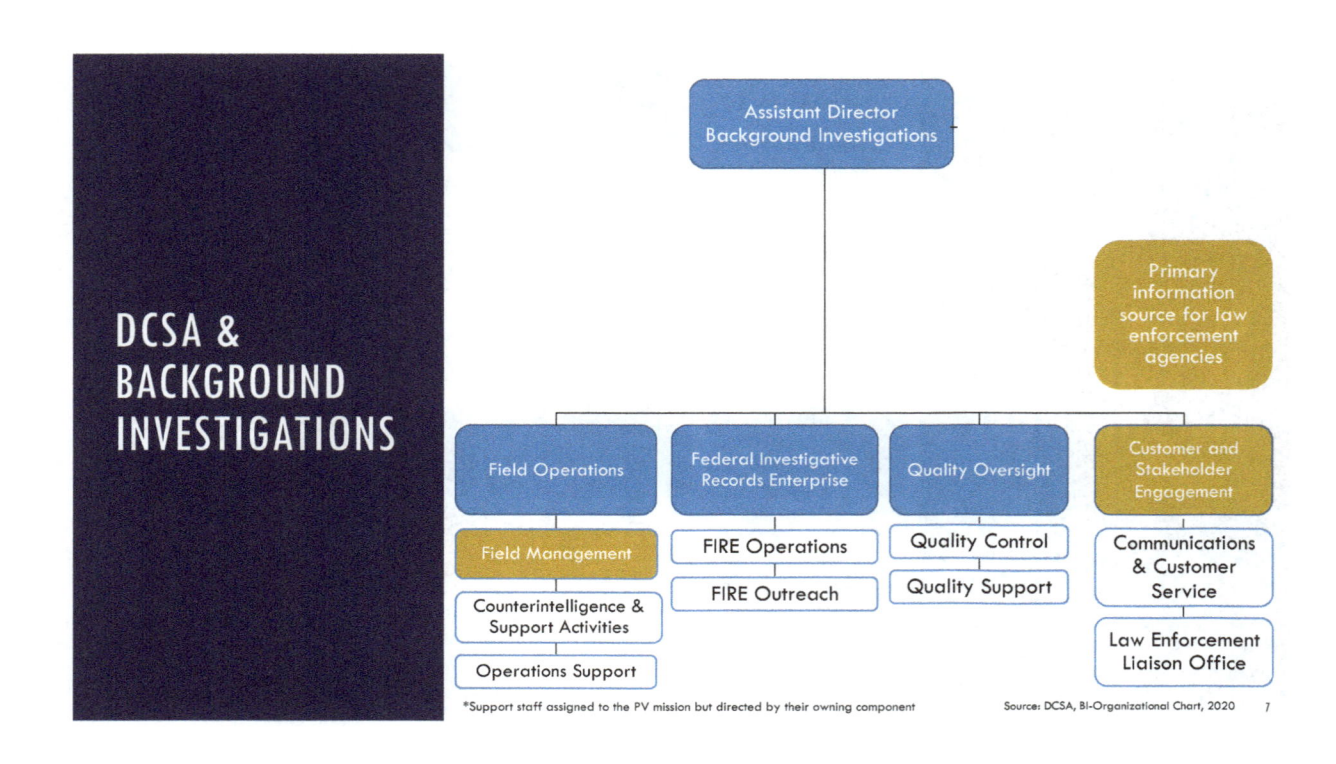

DCSA & BACKGROUND INVESTIGATIONS

Assistant Director Background Investigations

Primary information source for law enforcement agencies

- Field Operations
  - Field Management
  - Counterintelligence & Support Activities
  - Operations Support
- Federal Investigative Records Enterprise
  - FIRE Operations
  - FIRE Outreach
- Quality Oversight
  - Quality Control
  - Quality Support
- Customer and Stakeholder Engagement
  - Communications & Customer Service
  - Law Enforcement Liaison Office

*Support staff assigned to the PV mission but directed by their owning component

Source: DCSA, BI-Organizational Chart, 2020

DCSA & BACKGROUND INVESTIGATIONS

INITIATION
- 100+ agencies
- Applicant submits electronic questionnaire

INVESTIGATION
- Automated record checks
- Fieldwork

ADJUDICATION
- Report sent to initiating agency
- Agency reports determination
- Enrollment

Law enforcement–DCSA information sharing

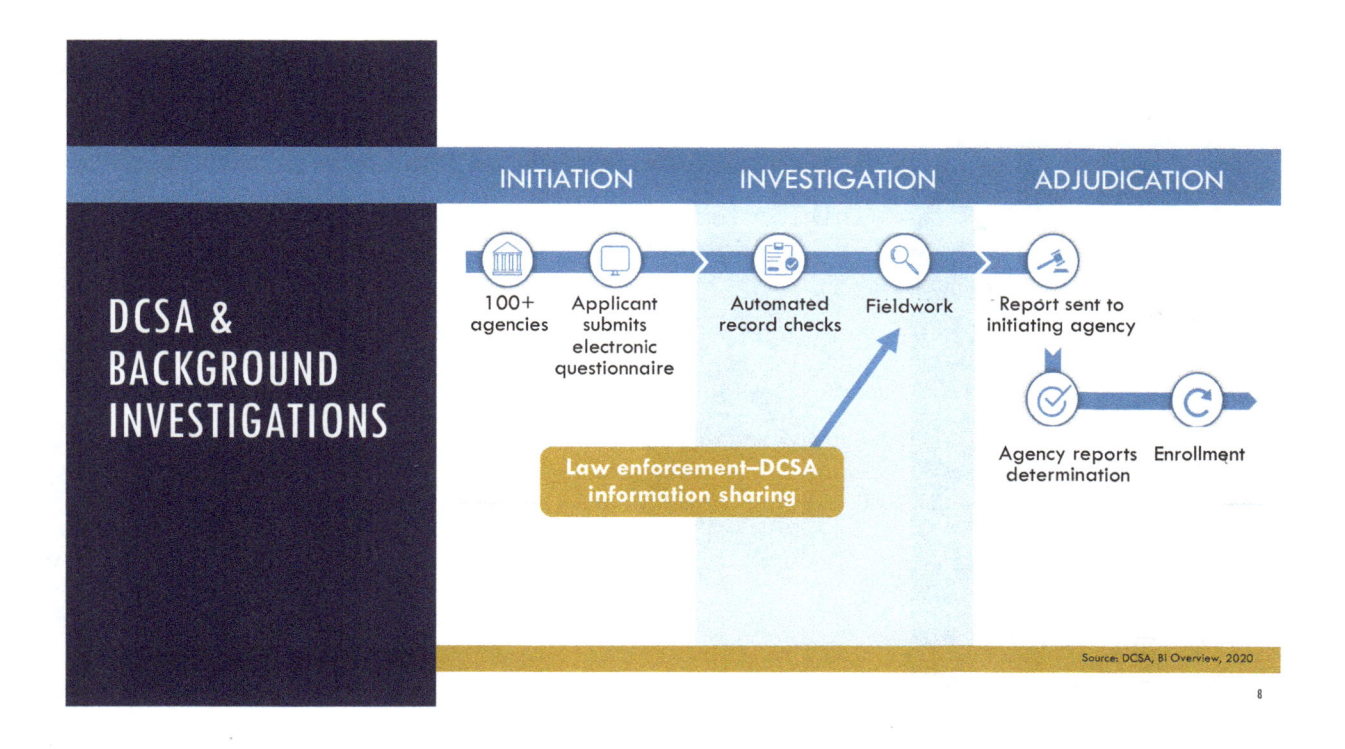

Source: DCSA, BI Overview, 2020

FEDERAL BACKGROUND INVESTIGATIVE FUNCTION TIMELINE

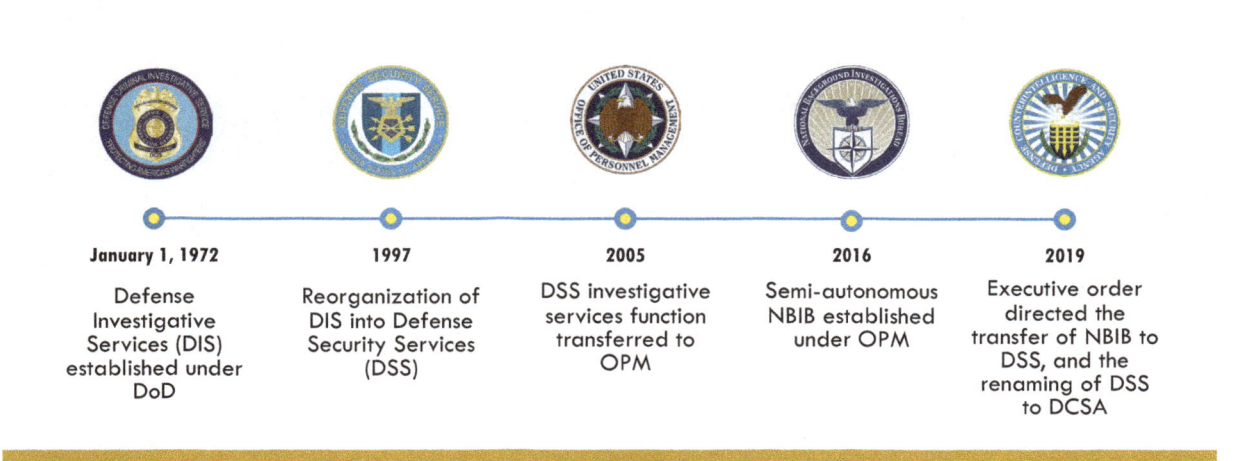

January 1, 1972 — Defense Investigative Services (DIS) established under DoD

1997 — Reorganization of DIS into Defense Security Services (DSS)

2005 — DSS investigative services function transferred to OPM

2016 — Semi-autonomous NBIB established under OPM

2019 — Executive order directed the transfer of NBIB to DSS, and the renaming of DSS to DCSA

WHO REPRESENTS DCSA?

DCSA federal investigators

DCSA contract investigators

AUTHORITIES

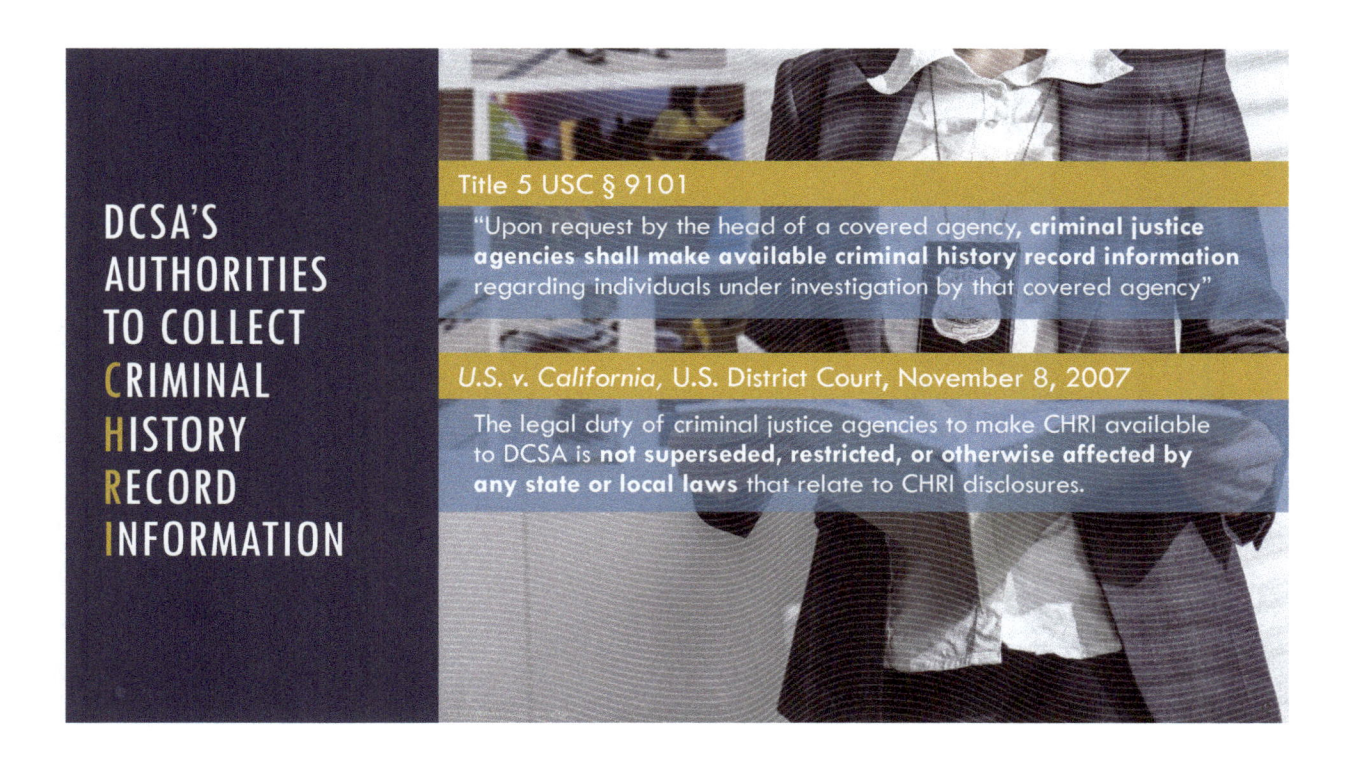

DCSA'S AUTHORITIES TO COLLECT CRIMINAL HISTORY RECORD INFORMATION

Title 5 USC § 9101

"Upon request by the head of a covered agency, **criminal justice agencies shall make available criminal history record information** regarding individuals under investigation by that covered agency"

U.S. v. California, U.S. District Court, November 8, 2007

The legal duty of criminal justice agencies to make CHRI available to DCSA is **not superseded, restricted, or otherwise affected by any state or local laws** that relate to CHRI disclosures.

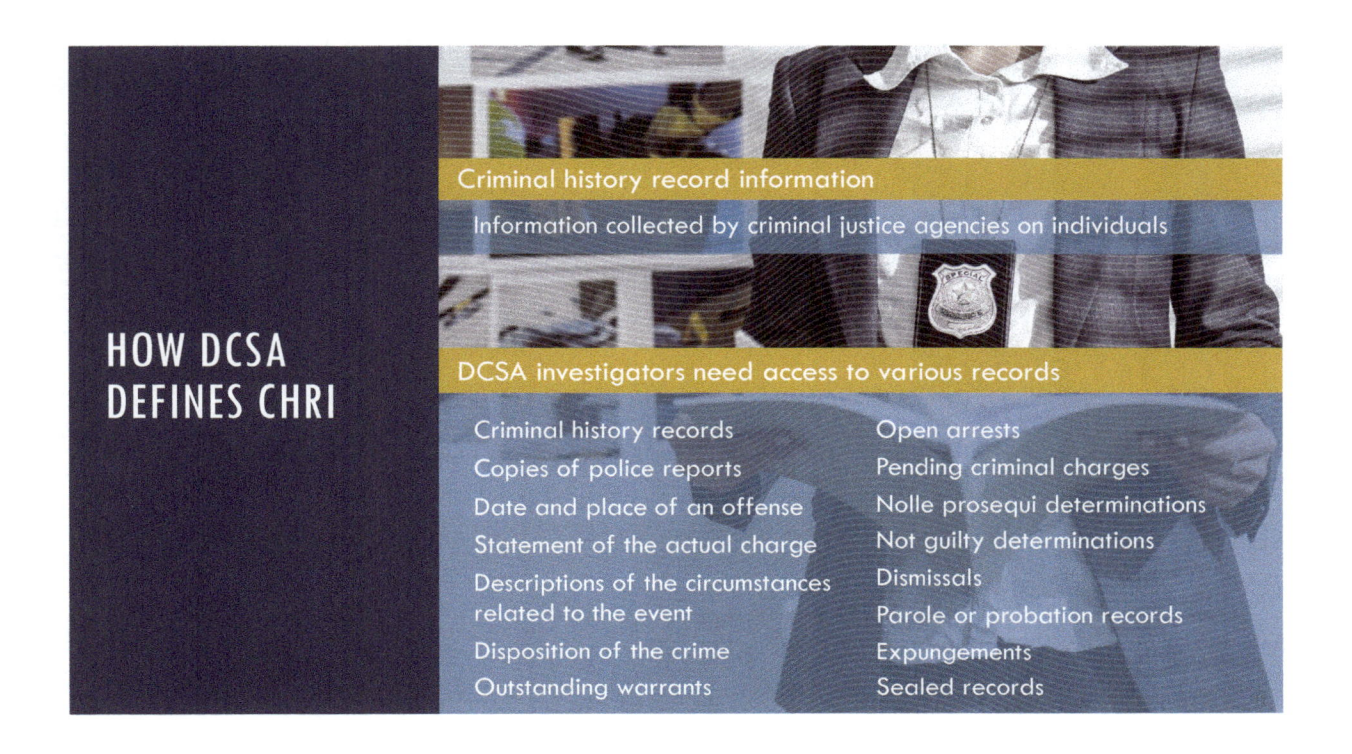

HOW DCSA DEFINES CHRI

Criminal history record information

Information collected by criminal justice agencies on individuals

DCSA investigators need access to various records

- Criminal history records
- Copies of police reports
- Date and place of an offense
- Statement of the actual charge
- Descriptions of the circumstances related to the event
- Disposition of the crime
- Outstanding warrants
- Open arrests
- Pending criminal charges
- Nolle prosequi determinations
- Not guilty determinations
- Dismissals
- Parole or probation records
- Expungements
- Sealed records

Criminal History Record Information Sharing with the Defense Counterintelligence and Security Agency

HOW DCSA COLLECTS CHRI FROM LAW ENFORCEMENT AGENCIES

Step 1 — Investigative request forms

HOW DCSA COLLECTS CHRI FROM LAW ENFORCEMENT AGENCIES

Step 1 — Investigative request forms

Step 2 — Investigator checks

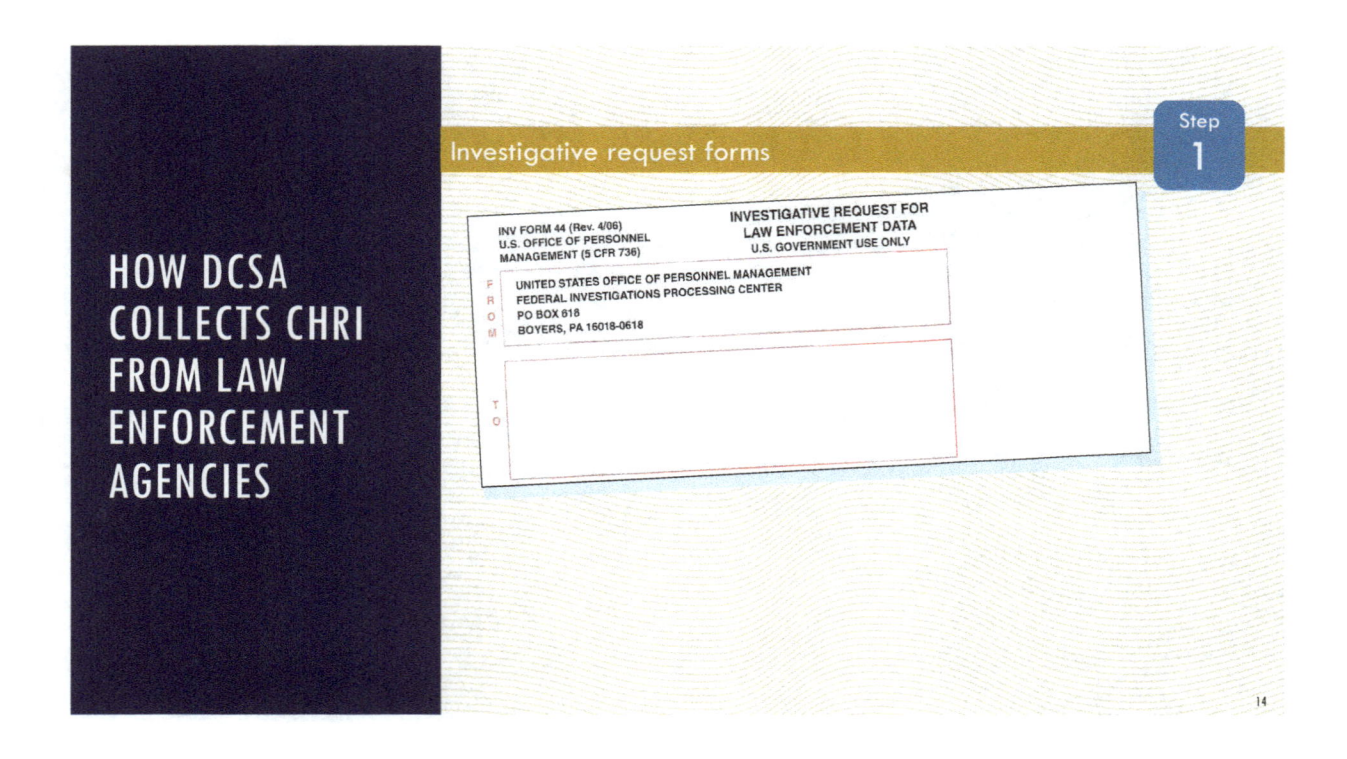

WHY YOU SHOULD SHARE INFORMATION WITH DCSA

WHY DCSA COLLECTS CHRI

- Uphold national security
- Required by law for all federal, state, local, territorial, and tribal entities
- Prevent threats to public safety

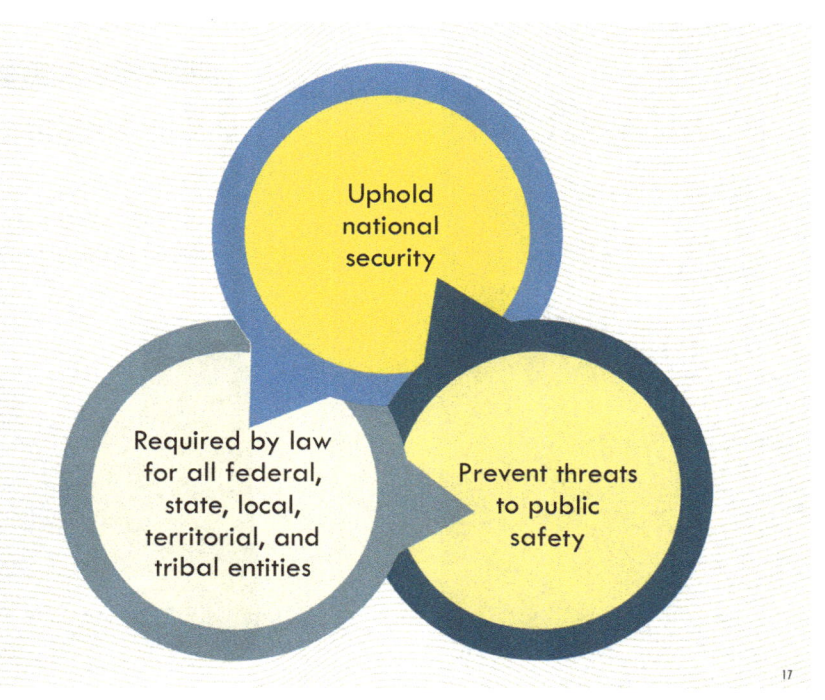

POTENTIAL CONSEQUENCES OF NOT SHARING CHRI WITH DCSA

Aaron Alexis, Navy Yard attack, 2013

POTENTIAL CONSEQUENCES OF NOT SHARING CHRI WITH DCSA

The Washington Post

National Security

Report says uncooperative local police stymie federal background security checks

DCSA CONTACTS

WHOM TO CONTACT

About a particular DCSA agent or investigator

DCSA Safety and Security Team
1-888-795-5673 between 7 a.m. and 4 p.m. EST, Monday–Friday

About how DCSA supports law enforcement agencies supplying CHRI

DCSA Law Enforcement Liaison Office
(202) 606-1606
DCSA.Law-Enforcement-Liason@mail.mil

Defense Counterintelligence and Security Agency
Attn: Law Enforcement Liaison Office
1900 E Street NW
Washington, DC 20415

About how to fill out and submit DCSA inquiry sheets

Federal Investigative Records Outreach
(724) 794-5612

US Department of Defense, Defense Counterintelligence and Security Agency
Attn: Federal Investigative Records Enterprise
Records Outreach P.O. Box 618
1137 Branchton Road
Boyers, PA 16018-0618

Questions?

DCSA BACKGROUND INVESTIGATIONS

Thank You

DCSA BACKGROUND INVESTIGATIONS

APPENDIX I

Posters

Each of the five posters provides brief distillations of key DCSA elements: its organization, personnel whom SLTT LEAs interact with, authorities, inquiry forms, and the CHRI sharing processes and procedures that are essential for DCSA to establish relationships and networks with SLTT jurisdictions. They are designed for wide dissemination and distribution (electronically or physically) and are constructed in a manner to allow for public display in SLTT LEA police and sheriffs' departments, correctional facilities, records offices, court clerks' offices, and professional conference booths to socialize SLTT LEA staff on essential CHRI sharing points. The posters are intended for placement in high-traffic and visibility areas so that key CHRI sharing points are reinforced in an accessible and eye-catching manner within SLTT LEA buildings and other public arenas where outreach is conducted.

Poster 1

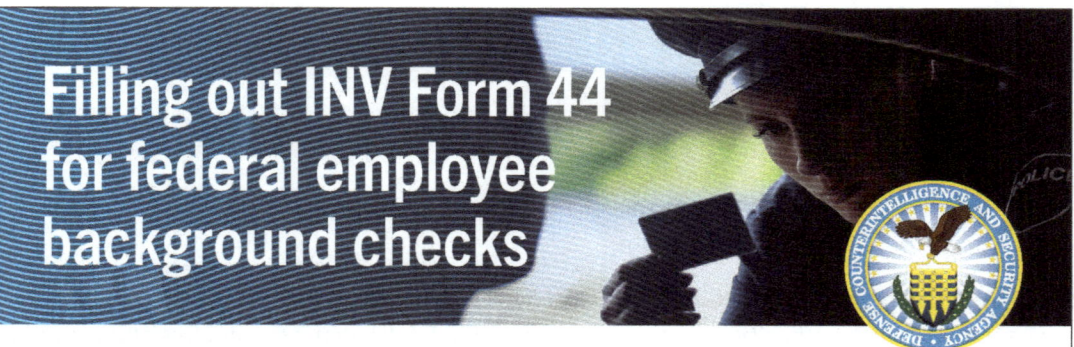

Filling out INV Form 44 for federal employee background checks

INV Form 44 is used for background investigations for federal personnel and the U.S. military that are conducted by the Defense Counterintelligence and Security Agency (DCSA)

INV FORM 44 (Rev. 4/06)
U.S. OFFICE OF PERSONNEL
MANAGEMENT (5 CFR 736)

INVESTIGATIVE REQUEST FOR
LAW ENFORCEMENT DATA
U.S. GOVERNMENT USE ONLY

FROM: UNITED STATES OFFICE OF PERSONNEL MANAGEMENT
FEDERAL INVESTIGATIONS PROCESSING CENTER
PO BOX 618
BOYERS, PA 16018-0618

Please complete the criminal history record information (CHRI) sections below and return the form as soon as possible. Return of this completed form to DCSA is urgent to prevent delays and to protect public safety and national security.

Questions? Contact the DCSA's Federal Investigative Records Enterprise (FIRE), Records Outreach, at (724) 794-5612.

Poster 2

Background Investigations and the Defense Counterintelligence and Security Agency (DCSA)

If DCSA Contacts Your Agency

When a DCSA Special Agent, Special Agent-in-Charge, or contract investigator contacts your law enforcement agency, please note the following:

Personnel can present badges/credentials, but these items cannot be photocopied.

DCSA agents and contractors need (and are authorized to receive) criminal history record information (CHRI) that includes the following:

- information about felonies, misdemeanors, traffic offenses, and other law violations
- detailed information about investigations, offenses, or any other pertinent contact with law enforcement.

If information resides at another law enforcement agency or court, please inform the investigator.

Whom You Can Contact at DCSA

Questions about verifying credentials or CHRI delays?

Local DCSA office: XXX-XXX-XXXX
Special Agent-in-Charge:
john.smith.civ@mail.mil

Questions about the CHRI request sheet, INV Form 44?

Federal Investigative Records Enterprise (FIRE),
Records Outreach
(724) 794-5612

U.S. Department of Defense
Defense Counterintelligence and Security Agency
Attn: Federal Investigative Records Enterprise,
Records Outreach
P.O. Box 618
1137 Branchton Road
Boyers, PA 16018-0618

PLEASE DO YOUR BEST TO MEET DCSA TIMELINES

CHRI collection is part of the background check for individuals applying for national security positions in the federal government and U.S. military.

Questions about an agent, contract investigator, or their authorization?

DCSA Safety and Security
(888) 795-5673
Mon.–Fri. 7 a.m.–4 p.m. ET

Photo credit: kali9/Getty Images

April 2022

Poster 3

How to Help with Background Investigations Conducted by the Defense Counterintelligence and Security Agency (DCSA)

If DCSA Contacts Your Agency

Personnel can present badges/credentials, but these items cannot be photocopied.

DCSA agents and contractors need (and are authorized to receive) criminal history record information (CHRI) that includes

- information about felonies, misdemeanors, traffic offenses, and other law violations
- detailed information about investigations, offenses, or any other pertinent contact with law enforcement.

If information resides at another law enforcement agency or court, please inform the investigator.

Whom You Can Contact at DCSA

About verifying credentials or CHRI delays

Local DCSA office: XXX-XXX-XXXX
Special Agent-in-Charge:
john.smith.civ@mail.mil

About the CHRI request sheet, INV Form 44

Federal Investigative Records Enterprise (FIRE), Records Outreach (724) 794-5612

U.S. Department of Defense
Defense Counterintelligence and Security Agency
Attn: Federal Investigative Records Enterprise, Records Outreach
P.O. Box 618
1137 Branchton Road
Boyers, PA 16018-0618

About an agent, investigator, or their authorization

DCSA Safety and Security
(888) 795-5673
Mon.–Fri. 7 a.m.–4 p.m. ET

PLEASE DO YOUR BEST TO MEET DCSA TIMELINES

CHRI collection is part of the background check for individuals applying for federal positions in national security and U.S. military branches.

Delays have implications for national security and public safety.

Photo credit: kali9/Getty Images/iStockphoto

April 2022

Poster 4

Responding to Defense Counterintelligence and Security Agency (DCSA) Requests

DCSA investigators may send you a form like the one below, via email or fax, as part of a background check on an applicant for federal employment. **Please supply this information and return this form to the investigator as soon as possible.**

Callouts pointing to the sample form:
- Subject of the background check
- Background on what DCSA needs and how the information was authorized
- How to verify that the request is legitimate
- Investigator and contact information
- Has your agency had contact with the subject? Please provide any arrests or police contacts on separate pages

---

DCSA is a federal agency that conducts background checks on individuals applying for national security positions in the federal government and U.S. military.

Please fill out and return this form promptly. Delays have implications for national security and public safety.

Poster 5

FEDERAL BACKGROUND CHECKS

If a DCSA investigator contacts your agency to help with a background check on an applicant for a national security position or the U.S. military, please note the following:

- Personnel can present badges/credentials, but they cannot be photocopied.
- DCSA personnel have timelines for completing background investigations, some of which hinge on the police, criminal, and traffic records that you provide. **PLEASE RESPOND AS SOON AS POSSIBLE.**

Local Contact Information

- If you have questions for the local DCSA office, such as verifying credentials, or experience issues or delays in providing criminal history record information, contact

  XXX-XXX-XXXX
  Special Agent-in-Charge:
  john@dcsa.mil

- If you have questions on the INV-44 sheet, contact
  Federal Investigative Records Enterprise (FIRE)
  (724) 794-5612

DEFENSE COUNTERINTELLIGENCE AND SECURITY AGENCY

Photo credit: Motortion/Getty Images/iStockphoto

April 2012

Abbreviations

CHRI	criminal history record information
COPS	Community Oriented Policing Services
COVID-19	coronavirus disease 2019
DCSA	Defense Counterintelligence and Security Agency
DoD	U.S. Department of Defense
FAQ	frequently asked questions
FLETC	Federal Law Enforcement Training Centers
LEA	law enforcement agency
LELO	Law Enforcement Liaison Office
NBIB	National Background Investigations Bureau
OPM	Office of Personnel Management
POC	point of contact
POST	Peace Officers Standards and Training
SAC	Special Agent-in-Charge
SLTT	state, local, tribal, and territorial
U.S.C.	U.S. Code

Bibliography

Beach, P., "Self-Directed Online Learning: A Theoretical Model for Understanding Elementary Teachers' Online Learning Experiences," *Teaching and Teacher Education*, Vol. 61, 2017, pp. 60–72. As of May 4, 2022:
https://doi.org/10.1016/j.tate.2016.10.007

Bellavita, C., ed., *How Public Organizations Work: Learning from Experience*, New York: Praeger, 1990.

Belur, J., W. Agnew-Pauley, B. McGinley, and L. Tompson, "A Systematic Review of Police Recruit Training Programmes," *Policing: A Journal of Policy and Practice*, Vol. 14, No. 1, 2020, pp. 76–90.

Birzer, M. L., "The Theory of Andragogy Applied to Police Training," *Policing: An International Journal of Police Strategies & Management*, 2003.

Birzer, M. L., and R. Tannehill, "A More Effective Training Approach for Contemporary Policing," *Police Quarterly*, Vol. 4, No. 2, 2001, pp. 233–252.

Blumberg, D. M., M. D. Schlosser, K. Papazoglou, S. Creighton, and C. C. Kaye, "New Directions in Police Academy Training: A Call to Action," *International Journal of Environmental Research and Public Health*, Vol. 16, No. 24, 2019, p. 4941.

Bourgerie, Erik J., written testimony for the President's Commission on Law Enforcement and the Administration of Justice, U.S. Department of Justice, May 13, 2020. As of May 10, 2022:
https://www.justice.gov/opa/page/file/1346316/download

Bradford, D., and J. E. Pynes, "Police Academy Training: Why Hasn't It Kept up with Practice?" *Police Quarterly*, Vol. 2, No. 3, 1999, pp. 283–301.

Cercone, K., "Characteristics of Adult Learners with Implications for Online Learning Design," *AACE Journal*, Vol. 16, No. 2, 2008, pp. 137–159.

Cleveland, G., and G. Saville, *Police PBL: Blueprint for the 21st Century*, U.S. Department of Justice, Office of Community Oriented Policing Services and Regional Community Policing Training Institute at Wichita State University, 2007. As of May 4, 2022:
https://cops.usdoj.gov/pdf/oswg/policepblbook2007.pdf

Code of Federal Regulations, Title 48, Section 1.106, OMB approval under the Paperwork Reduction Act.

Cochran, C., and S. Brown, "Andragogy and the Adult Learner," in K. Flores, K. D. Kirstein, C. E. Schieber, and S. G. Olswang, *Supporting the Success of Adult and Online Students*, Scotts Valley, Calif.: CreateSpace, 2016. As of May 4, 2022:
http://repository.cityu.edu/handle/20.500.11803/594

Community Oriented Policing Services Training, "E-Learning," webpage, undated. As of May 10, 2022:
https://copstrainingportal.org/elearning/

Connecticut State Police Officer Standards and Training Council, "In-Service Training Courses," webpage, 2021. As of May 4, 2022:
https://portal.ct.gov/POST/Field-Services-Training-Courses/In-Service-Training-Courses

Connolly, J., "Rethinking Police Training," *Police Chief*, Vol. 75, No. 11, 2008.

DCSA—*See* Defense Counterintelligence and Security Agency.

Defense Counterintelligence and Security Agency, "Adjudication," webpage, undated. As of May 10, 2022:
https://www.dcsa.mil/mc/pv/dod_caf/adjudications/

Donohue, R. H., and N. E. Kruis, "Comparing the Effects of Academy Training Models on Recruit Competence: Does Curriculum Instruction Type Matter?" *Policing: An International Journal*, 2020.

Federal Law Enforcement Training Centers, *Strategic Plan, 2018–2022*, Glynco, Ga., undated. As of May 4, 2022:
https://www.fletc.gov/site-page/strategic-plan

Goggins, B., and D. DeBacco, *Challenges and Promising Practices for Disposition Reporting*, report from the 2017 SEARCH Winter Membership Group Meeting, Phoenix, Ariz., January 24–26, 2017.

Heckscher, C., *The Collaborative Enterprise: Managing Speed and Complexity in Knowledge-Based Businesses*, New Haven, Conn.: Yale University Press, 2007.

International Association of Directors of Law Enforcement Standards and Training, "Academy Policies and Procedures in Time of Pandemic," webpage, undated. As of May 4, 2022:
https://www.iadlest.org/news/covid-academy-policies

INTERPOL, "INTERPOL Launches Virtual Academy to Support Police Learning During COVID 19," press release, April 29, 2020. As of May 4, 2022:
https://www.interpol.int/en/News-and-Events/News/2020/
INTERPOL-launches-Virtual-Academy-to-support-police-learning-during-COVID-19

Kolb, D. A., *Experiential Learning: Experience as the Source of Learning and Development*, Englewood Cliffs, N.J.: Prentice-Hall, 1984.

Kolb, D. A., and L. H. Lewis, "Facilitating Experiential Learning: Observations and Reflections," *New Directions for Continuing Education*, Vol. 30, 1986, pp. 99–107.

Knowles, M. S., *Self-Directed Learning: A Guide for Learners and Teachers*, New York: Association Press, 1975.

Lauritz, L. E., E. Åström, C. Nyman, and M. Klingvall, "Police Students' Learning Preferences, Suitable Responses from the Learning Environment," *Policing: A Journal of Policy and Practice*, Vol. 7, No. 2, 2013, pp. 195–203.

Lewis, L. H., and C. J. Williams, "Experiential Learning: Past and Present," *New Directions for Adult and Continuing Education, 1994*, Vol. 62, 1994, pp. 5–16.

Lowry, C. M., "Supporting and Facilitating Self-Directed Learning," *ERIC Digest*, No. 93, 1989.

Marenin, O., "Police Training for Democracy," *Police Practice and Research*, Vol. 5, No. 2, 2004, pp. 107–123.

McCoy, M. R., "Teaching Style and the Application of Adult Learning Principles by Police Instructors," *Policing: An International Journal of Police Strategies & Management*, 2006.

McGrath, V., "Reviewing the Evidence on How Adult Students Learn: An Examination of Knowles' Model of Andragogy," *Adult Learner: The Irish Journal of Adult and Community Education*, Vol. 99, 2009.

Merriam, S. B., "Andragogy and Self-Directed Learning: Pillars of Adult Learning Theory," *New Directions for Adult and Continuing Education*, Vol. 89, 2001.

Merriam, S. B., and L. L. Bierema, *Adult Learning: Linking Theory and Practice*, San Francisco: Jossey-Bass, 2014.

Merriam, S. B., and R. S. Caffarella, *Learning in Adulthood*, 2nd ed., San Francisco: Jossey-Bass, 1999.

Oliva, J. R., and M. T. Compton, "What Do Police Officers Value in the Classroom? A Qualitative Study of the Classroom Social Environment in Law Enforcement Education," *Policing: An International Journal of Police Strategies & Management*, 2010.

Ozuah, P. O., "First, There Was Pedagogy and Then Came Andragogy," *Einstein Journal of Biology and Medicine*, Vol. 21, No. 2, pp. 83–87. As of May 4, 2022:
https://www.researchgate.net/publication/255636828_First_There_Was_Pedagogy_And_Then_Came_Andragogy

PoliceOne Academy, homepage, undated. As of May 4, 2022:
https://www.policeoneacademy.com

Public Law 116-92, National Defense Authorization Act for Fiscal Year 2020, December 20, 2019.

Rojek, J., J. Grieco, B. Meade, and D. Parsons, *National Survey on Officer Safety Training: Findings and Implications*, Washington, D.C.: National Police Foundation, 2020.

Stoika, D., moderator, "President's Commission on Law Enforcement and the Administration of Justice," conference call transcript, U.S. Department of Justice, May 13, 2020. As of May 4, 2022:
https://www.justice.gov/ag/page/file/1278886/download

U.S. Code, Title 5, Section 9101, Access to criminal history records for national security and other purposes.

U.S. Department of Defense, Defense Visual Information Distribution Service, *DCSA ACCESS Magazine*, online portal, undated-a. As of May 10, 2022:
https://www.dvidshub.net/publication/899/dcsa-access-magazine

U.S. Department of Defense, Defense Visual Information Distribution Service, "Defense Counterintelligence and Security Agency," webpage, undated-b. As of May 10, 2022:
https://www.dvidshub.net/unit/dcsa

U.S. Department of Justice, Office of Community Oriented Policing Services, "E-Learning," webpage, undated. As of May 4, 2022:
https://copstrainingportal.org/elearning/

U.S. Department of Justice, U.S. Attorney's Office, District of Columbia, "U.S. Attorney's Office Closes Investigation Involving Fatal Shooting of Aaron Alexis No Charges to Be Filed Against Officers Who Responded to Mass Murders at Washington Navy Yard," press release, August 27, 2014. As of May 11, 2022:
https://www.justice.gov/usao-dc/pr/us-attorney-s-office-closes-investigation-involving-fatal-shooting-aaron-alexis-no

U.S. Office of Personnel Management, *Investigator's Handbook*, Federal Investigative Services Division, July 2007, Not available to the general public.

U.S. Office of Personnel Management, *Federal Investigative Standards*, v.5, September 14, 2020, Not available to the general public.

Vonderwell, S., and S. Turner, "Active Learning and Preservice Teachers' Experiences in an Online Course: A Case Study," *Journal of Technology and Teacher Education*, Vol. 13, No. 1, 2005, pp. 65–84. As of May 4, 2022:
http://learntechlib.org/p/18892/

Wambeke, B. W., B. E. Barry, and J. C. Bruhl, *Teaching Model as a Living Document*, 2017 ASEE Annual Conference and Exposition, Columbus, Ohio, June 24–28, 2017. As of May 4, 2022:
https://peer.asee.org/teaching-model-as-a-living-document

Werth, E. P., "Scenario Training in Police Academies: Developing Students' Higher-Level Thinking Skills," *Police Practice and Research*, Vol. 12, No. 4, 2011, pp. 325–340.

Lightning Source UK Ltd.
Milton Keynes UK
UKHW050657031222
413115UK00009B/71